The Elk Mystique

Mike Lapinski

The Elk Mystique

Mike Lapinski

Copyright 1998 by Mike Lapinski

ISBN 0-912299-73-8

STONEYDALE PRESS PUBLISHING COMPANY
523 Main Street • P.O. Box 188
Stevensville, Montana 59870
Phone: 406-777-2729

Table of Contents

Dedication

This book is dedicated to those tireless men who created from nothing an irresistible force of humanity for the conservation of elk and elk habitat. And in championing the cause of this magnificent animal, they also led America into a new dimension of natural resource stewardship.

Those men are the Rocky Mountain Elk Foundation's founding fathers — Charlie Decker, Bob Munson, Bill Munson and Dan Bull. The glowing status of the elk today, and conservation in general, is due in large part to their courage and determination.

But lest we forget, this book also recognizes the Elk Foundation's fallen warriors, Wallace Pate, Phil Tawney, and Ken Grant — plus a wounded warrior, Hugh Hogle. They took up the staff and banner, and strove forward until they could go no more. Now it's our turn.

Prologue

First Contact

The first rays of autumn sunlight spray across the frost-burnt aspens in the secluded Montana backcountry basin and instantly turn the world a translucent amber gold. Senses already rendered visually acute are further heightened by the pungent aroma of fresh earth and dead leaves wafting through the crisp, thin air.

I slip forward silently, hesitantly. Even in the cold, my blood runs hot, and a trickle of nerve-induced sweat cascades down my rib cage, sending an involuntary shiver down my spine. The tremors increase until my entire body quivers with a mixture of anticipation and trepidation.

With trembling hands, I raise the elk call to my lips. The sound I emit is a poor excuse for a rutting bull elk's challenging bugle, but I'm hopeful. My ears strain for that wonderfully hollow, musical response — full of power and fury.

Time stands still. The pressures and petty urgencies of civilized life dissolve into strangely inconsequential trivia in comparison to my primal need to relate to this unknown rut-crazed denizen holed up in his backcountry lair just out of sight.

The forest becomes hushed, almost foreboding. With bated breath, I wait. And I tremble. I close my eyes and urgently whisper, "Come on, come on. Answer me!" ..... And then it comes.

Mike Lapinski

The Elk Mystique

The awesome spectacle of a huge bull elk in rut charging forward with head held high and mighty rack of swept back antlers glistening in the autumn sun has a way of capturing your attention. First-time urban visitors to elk country who thought the elk to be nothing more than a big deer, are stunned by the enormous mass and fluid movement of an animal so large that its heavy hoofbeats actually shake the ground.

Maybe it's the primal man hidden within our civilized psyche that irrevocably draws folks from throughout the world to enter into communion with the elk and experience nature in its most simple, raw, yet beautiful, form. Whatever the reason, every summer and fall a small army of elk enthusiasts is lured to elk country to witness the magical world of the American elk.

The fall spectacle of the elk rut, combined with the vivid colors of autumn, is an especially precious time of year to observe and photograph the bulls as they joust and vie for the females, and then pose for the long lines of photographers eagerly capturing their every move.

I've witnessed a lot of various phenomena in the natural world, but the adrenalin level and excitement that literally ripples through the air among both elk and man during the rutting season combine to create one of the most inspiring and enjoyable outdoor happenings that I have ever experienced. In fact, I count the days between Septembers, so ingrained in my soul is this very special event.

The famous world traveled photographer Leonard Lee Rue said it best when he quipped, "If I'm not in Yellowstone National Park in September for the elk rut, I get homesick!"

The most awesome elk rutting action I've ever experienced occurs in Canada's Banff National Park. The rutting elk there become very aggressive and just about take over the small town of Jasper. Dominant bulls herd their cows right down main street and often choose the school playground to bed down for the day.

In fact, travel agencies book charters for visitors from throughout the world to come to Banff and experience the thrill and excitement of the elk rut in fall. However, this experience does have its drawbacks for some foreign visitors who are unfamiliar with the testy mood of the bull elk in rut.

he ominous figure floating through the murky light of dawn becomes more familiar, but
o less surreal. Out here — in the wild — the roles are reversed. I am but a human,
hile he is a mighty king commanding respect. I am filled with awe and wonder, while
e is filled with fury and power. I dare not breathe, while he dares not be silent.

*...tlers glistening in the early morning sun, head held high and challenging the world —
...e bull elk in rut stirs the primal man within us.*

The Rocky Mountain grandeur, combined with the graceful beauty and raw power of the elk, create an ethereal atmosphere.

One morning, I drove around a corner in Jasper and spotted a Japanese tourist desperately clinging to a telephone pole ten feet above the sidewalk, with a huge seven-point herd bull down below angrily shaking his mighty rack of antlers at the wide-eyed man.

I eased my car forward and beeped the horn to spook the elk away. My guess is that the bull took that as a challenge because he lowered his antlers and charged. My car barely outran the huge brute as we both sped down the highway in this absurd encounter.

The man up the pole? Instead of being scared stiff, he considered the entire (and potentially dangerous) encounter to be a thoroughly exhilarating affair. He was greeted by his touring group with applause and enjoyed somewhat of a celebrity status afterwards!

But it is interesting to note that many elk enthusiasts also choose to visit elk country in the summer to observe the drama of life and death in the elk herd, as the cows give birth to beautiful spotted calves, followed closely by a succession of predators who prey on these defenseless young. It may be harsh and seemingly cruel to the casual visitor, but to the elk lover, it remains a sobering, though uplifting, experience because in the end, the elk herd continues to maintain its existence and grow.

So what is this mystique about the elk that has led the relatively new Rocky Mountain Elk Foundation to swell in membership to well over 115,000 worldwide in just over a decade? Surely, the elk is not the only species of interest. America is blessed with an abundance of wildlife ranging from the urban whitetail deer to the taciturn grizzly bear. However, it is the Rocky Mountain elk that most outdoor enthusiasts have come to associate with a wild and free America.

This is no doubt due to the wild, pristine environment where the elk is found, and yet it is still very accessible for elk watchers. Add to that, the elk's huge size, regal beauty and vocal, cordial nature — and you have an animal that has literally captured the imagination of outdoor America.

One of the greatest attractions of the elk is its unique personality. Unlike the furtive deer, which is frightened of its own shadow, both male and female elk carry themselves with a dignity that is remarkable. Even the amateur photographer is often able to capture this stately nature of the elk on film.

As knowledge of the elk, its habits, and its habitat has become known among elk lovers, their awareness that elk once roamed over virtually all of America has spawned a grassroots drive to return the elk to much of its former range. Today, you don't have to drive all the way to Yellowstone National Park to hear the haunting bugle of the mighty bull elk in rut. Small, but flourishing elk herds are popping up in the midwest, the east, and even in the south as the elk is slowly reintroduced into its historical range.

Elk in Kentucky? Yes! How about Pennsylvania? You better believe it! Even in Arkansas? In Kansas? Wonderful, isn't it!

Travelers come from all over the world to view the mighty bull elk in his pristine environment.

Chapter One

Elk Country

Sheer rock walls rise skyward and snow capped mountain peaks literally touch the clouds. Below, the rock precipices give way to alpine meadows covered with a velvet-like carpet of soft grass and resplendent in a profusion of wildflowers.

The air up here is clean and clear, but thin, due to the high elevation. And always in the high country, the morning air has a crispness to it that hints of frost even in the summer months. The morning sun burns surprisingly hot, and quickly sizzles the dripping morning dew into a steamy, humid vapor that hugs the low spots in the meadows for an hour and then vanishes, leaving behind a brilliant sun drenched landscape.

The fragrant scent of beargrass and wildflowers mingles with the pungent aroma of over-ripened huckleberries. The smell of fresh earth and ferns add to the olfactory messages floating in the soft summer breeze.

Everywhere, ice cold streams and waterfalls gush snow-melted waters. The gurgles of brooks, rushing streams, and pounding waterfalls create a cacophony of muffled sound that is constant and interrupted only by the shrill cry of a hawk hunting for a plump, furry pica, or the raucous protest of a crow.

Farther down the mountainside, fingers of stunted spruce and alpine fir trees separated by small meadows dot the landscape before ending in a sea of coniferous trees. Stands of massive ponderosa pine, Douglas fir and tamarack trees over a hundred feet tall loom skyward, with whip-like lodgepole pine and billowing groves of dainty aspens filling in the gaps below.

This in itself is enough grandeur to satiate any human visitor, but there is more. Like precious jewels on a crown, elk dot the pristine mountain landscape and lend a surreal touch to an already peaceful land.

Cow elk graze peacefully on the lush meadow grass, while calves romp playfully throughout the herd, stopping only long enough to nurse from mother. The bulls lay in bachelor groups in the shade, eyes closed and chewing their cuds.

Among the dozing elk lie old rodent-gnawed antlers shed years ago by ancestors of today's herd and they now create a convenient basket for wildflowers.

nowcapped peaks in the background and the mighty bull elk in the foreground — surely his must be ELK COUNTRY!

Weather-cracked bones bleached white lie scattered throughout the land and attest to the fact that the perfect cycle of nature is not without a price.

This is elk country in the Rocky Mountains. There is no other place on earth that can compare with these various elements that combine to create one of the most breathtaking sights in the world.

This is the type of habitat that elk choose to live in. While there are millions of acres of wilderness throughout the West, only about ten percent is elk habitat. And within that habitat suitable for elk, there are found specific pockets of terrain where most of the elk prefer to live, called prime habitat.

It is an unnerving experience for the first time visitor to the West, when he or she gazes upon miles of rolling forest and mountains and sees not only an absence of elk, but also no tracks or droppings. Fortunately, elk are easily located if you know what prime habitat consists of and where elk prefer to live.

Elk are semi-wilderness dwellers, especially in areas where they are hunted or where civilization has encroached upon historic elk habitat. Even in our national parks where they are protected, most of the elk prefer to stay away from people and civilization in general. This is one of the personality traits of an elk that identifies it as such a unique animal.

Sure, there will always be a few cows that linger just outside of town, but

Rodent-gnawed antlers and bleached bones lie scattered throughout elk country and attest to the fact that the perfect cycle of nature does not come without a price.

most of the elk will stay as far away from towns, vehicles and barking dogs as possible.

The majority of western land is lower country where dense forest grows, and less nourishing grass is found. And the grasslands that exist are fenced and guarded jealously by ranchers. That fact, combined with the tendency for towns and human populations to be concentrated in these lower elevations, usually eliminates these vast areas as suitable elk habitat.

Generally, in mountainous terrain the elk will be found in the upper third of the mountain during summer and fall, above the dense forest where scant grass and brush grows. Of course, a few elk will always be found at this mid-level of the mountain, but these elk are usually just passing through from one area of prime habitat to another.

Specifically, elk prefer that zone on a mountain where the dense forest begins to give way to small meadows. This is called subalpine terrain; it is that special place where the elk can find feed, water and shelter. But most important, it is usually a long distance from civilization.

In the southern Rocky Mountain states such as New Mexico and Arizona, the majority of elk still prefer the upper reaches of the mountains. However, the

Elk are slowly reclaiming much of the open Plains country. This semi-open rolling hills habitat had been historically preferred by the elk before the encroachment of civilization forced them into the thickets and mountains.

mid-elevations in the Southwest mountains are free from the dense forests of the northern Rockies. These southern mid-elevation forests are comprised mostly of scattered bull pine, which allow enough sun to penetrate their canopy and much grass grows. In these areas, a good population of elk exists.

This bull pine habitat does furnish ample feed, but it often lacks enough heavy cover to make the elk feel secure, so at first light, they often migrate for miles up to the higher country where the vegetation and tree cover is thicker and

In mountainous terrain, most elk will be found in the upper third of the mountain in summer and fall, where the heavy forest gives way to small meadows.

they feel more secure in their day beds. In evening, they make the long trip back down to the bull pine flats to feed and frolic.

I spent some time in one of these areas of New Mexico, and I was amazed at the stamina that these transient elk possessed. I had spent most of my time with elk of the northern Rockies, who often moved less than a half mile between feed, bed and cover. But these elk of the southern Rockies always seemed impatient and on the move, and at the brisk rate that they traveled (about 7 mph), I was always left gasping and unable to keep up with their daily routines, which seemed hectic to me, but nonchalant to them.

While most of the elk in America inhabit the Rocky Mountains, there are large populations of elk that inhabit other areas which suit their requirements of food, shelter, water and solitude. Large expanses of semi-arid sagebrush and juniper rolling hills in the eastern foothills of the southern Rockies also harbor large elk herds.

Actually, this semi-open plains country was the historic preferred habitat of the elk. The encroachment of civilization drove the elk to adapt to their new mountainous terrain. But given the security and seclusion, elk like this open rolling terrain.

Much of this habitat exists in national forests or on state land, but several huge private cattle ranches also tolerate the elk on their property and allow their cattle and the elk to mingle freely.

The problem with much of this semi-arid habitat is that it lacks ample feed and water. Fortunately, the long-legged elk are capable of traveling remarkable distances, and it is not unusual for an elk herd to bed down in the high juniper covered hills where they feel secure, but then migrate down five miles or more to grass lands to feed, then travel another five miles to a distant water hole to guzzle water, before making the long trek back up to their bedding areas in the juniper thickets.

The exact opposite environment exists on the other side of the Rockies, along the Coastal Mountains of Washington, Oregon and northern California where the subspecies of elk, called the Roosevelt, exists in the rain forests along the coast of the Pacific Ocean. This is a steep, rain-drenched land of dense forest and impenetrable brush where the elk often move less than a half mile during their daily travels.

Though the terrain in elk country may vary greatly, there is still a special beauty to all of it. True, the pristine high country of the Rockies has a magical, jewel-like quality, but the softer environment of the rolling semi-arid foothills of the Southwest has its own allure that makes a visitor want to hike through the gently rolling hills all day. Even the Coastal Mountain Range along the Pacific Rim holds an exotic charm within its damp, moss covered forests.

The common denominator that transforms any of these lands from picturesque, to special, is the elk herd that dwells there. In fact, such a land is even given a special name. It's called ELK COUNTRY!

Chapter Two

The Elk of Pilgrim America

The America that the first European settlers encountered back in the 16th century was a vast sea of hardwood forests. Numerous species of oak, along with a mixture of beech, maple, hickory and ash covered the land in an endless, billowing canopy of green trees. Only along the fringes of lakes or streams, or where wildfires had burned, were grassy openings to be found.

This enormous forest stretched the length of the eastern seaboard and penetrated westward into the heartland a thousand miles, through present-day Iowa and Indiana, before finally dwindling in the heat and parched earth of the Great Plains. This was the natural forested environment of Pilgrim America.

Besides the strangeness of the land, early settlers were met with a plethora of strange and unknown fowl, furbearers and large animals. The turkey was a new and welcome discovery because of its excellent table fare. Another unique animal, called the beaver, created dams wherever it lived and provided fur for clothing in the cold winter months.

The new arrivals in the Virginia colony also encountered a medium sized deer of great speed and agility, eventually called the Virginia whitetail deer. There were many other wondrous wildlife discoveries during those formative years of America's early settlements, such as poisonous reptiles and a myriad of new birds and small mammals.

However, there was a large beast that many of the Pilgrims, to their surprise, did recognize, given the tendency for this new land to harbor mostly unfamiliar wildlife species. The animal closely resembled the European red deer, and many of them immediately called them stags, though observers back then did notice differences. This new animal, at about a half ton, was quite a bit larger than the 600 pound red deer, and its color was more tan than red. The male's musical mating call also differed from the guttural roar of the male red deer.

The naming of this giant deer became quite an issue for the early colonists. Other species of wildlife were easy to name because they were new, and a simple consensus was all that was needed to label, for instance, the Virginia whitetail deer. (It was first observed in Virginia.) But among many of the learned colonists, there erupted much disagreement concerning the proper name for the giant deer-

The Pilgrims discovered many new and strange creatures in the New World. But one large animal they immediately recognized from the Old World was the elk.

like animal that roamed the eastern hardwoods.

Many observers called the males the common red deer name of "stag." But others, noting the marked differences between the red deer and this new animal, called it, "American red deer," or "Canada stag." The big problem occurred when some colonists began misnaming it "elk."

In Europe, the term "elk" referred to the European moose. No doubt, this name was used because the larger size of this new animal more approximated the size of the European moose, than the smaller red deer. The term "elk" seemed to gather the consensus — until the American moose was discovered.

Many settlers adopted the Algonquin Indian name of "moosh" for this large ungulate. Soon, a great controversy erupted about the proper name for this giant deer-like animal that resembled, but did not replicate, any specific species.

There were so many names and opinions bantered around through those early seventeenth century colonist years, that it was often difficult to tell exactly what species of animals were being encountered. For instance, some New England colonists used the name, "grey moose," to refer to the elk. Others called both species "moose," and differentiated between them as simply "black moose" and "brown moose."

By the beginning of the 18th century, the misnomer of "elk" was the common term used. However, that was also the period when great naturalists of the world were laying the groundwork for most of our academic natural history. They painstakingly documented, with precise biological accuracy, each new species found in the New World. So it is understandable why they would pull their hair out when ignorant settlers referred to this new animal as an elk. To a dedicated scientist of natural history, it was pure butchery to use the term "elk."

The controversy simmered until the great explorers, Lewis & Clark, made their epic journey into the unknown heart of America. Their diaries were received as gospel among naturalists, and since they used the term "elk" to describe the giant deer, that name has generally, though grudgingly, been accepted.

Stubborn naturalists squirmed at this mis-name. Finally, they settled on the name "Wapiti." This is the Shoshone Indian name for the elk, and means "white rump." Though never completely usurping the elk as a descriptive term, the name Wapiti is now used by many academics to deliver a biologically accurate name for the American elk, or is it moose, or is it...!

Surprisingly, this confusion carries on even today. I was visiting Lolo Hot Springs in western Montana, where Lewis & Clark stopped to soak weary muscles in the natural hot mineral pools, when I met two quite proper British tourists. They gushed about the beauty of the land and its wildlife. They were particularly excited about an elk that they'd seen at the pond beside the main lodge where we sat chatting.

I thought it was odd that an elk would come down to the marshy pond right next to a busy highway, when most other elk were far away in their summer subalpine habitat. I joined my new friends near the pond the next morning. As we watched, you guessed it, a huge moose ambled into the pond and dipped its head under water to feed on succulent water lilies.

Fortunately, I understood where their confusion came from and patiently

This painting illustrates how early American artists continued to be influenced by the more familiar European red deer physique.

explained the history of this naming problem. After I'd explained it in thorough detail, the man finally nodded in understanding and capsulized my long-winded conversation with the quip, "Even though it was a biological elk we saw, over here it's a moose!" Hmm!

This confusion over exactly what to call the American elk also surfaced a few years ago while I watched a television episode of *Wild Kingdom*, which featured Marlin Perkins studying, chasing down, and capturing elk in the western United States. During the program, Mr. Perkins often referred to the male elk as "stags."

Maybe three hundred years ago, the term "stag" to describe the American elk would have been valid. But through the years, scientists and wildlife biologists have concurred that the proper term for the male American elk is a "bull."

While the controversy over what name to call the American elk died down, the biological classification of the elk was just heating up. Many early naturalists of the 18th century doubted that the Eurasian red deer and the American elk could reproduce fertile offspring, a prerequisite for including two similar animals into a "single-species" (subspecies) category. For instance, the mule deer and whitetail deer are classified as subspecies because they have the capability of producing fertile offspring.

Even the great naturalist, Murie, sided with those who believed the isolation and physical differences between the Eurasian red deer and the American Elk precluded their having the capability to produce fertile offspring. Hence, early naturalists tended to classify the American elk as *Cervus canadensis*, as opposed to *Cervus elaphus*, the Eurasian red deer's biological classification.

In the 1850's both red deer and American elk were transplanted to New Zealand in separate locations, and naturalists watched intently for any unions to occur. To almost everyone's surprise, elk and red deer did hybridize and produce fertile offspring.

This produced a major shakeup in the world of naturalists, and eventually led to the reclassification of the American elk and Eurasian red deer as the same species, *Cervus elaphus*.

Elk purists shrugged at all this scientific jostling. It mattered little to them what the American elk was called, as long as the bloodlines were kept uncontaminated by red deer genes — an impossibility considering their ocean-wide isolation.

From the hybridized mess in New Zealand, they wanted nothing to do with

The American elk on the left, at 800 pounds, dwarfs the 500 pound European red deer on the right. In addition, the American elk's antlers are symmetrical and swept back and its body color is tan, while the red deer's antlers tend to be straighter with a crown of points at the end. Illustration by Dennis Althoff.

trying to figure out whether a particular animal was an elk, or a hybrid. Amid howls of protest, red deer were allowed to be imported onto game farms in America a few decades ago. Proponents of this action countered that game farms were strictly regulated by state wildlife agencies, and literally no possibility existed for red deer and native elk to interbreed.

Unfortunately, that was not the case, when several red deer escaped from a game farm in western Montana. Most were quickly dispatched, but not all animals were accounted for. A few years ago, an elk harvested in the Lewis & Clark National Forest south of Helena, Montana, was found to carry red deer genes.

And a few years ago, three elk killed in the wilds of Wyoming's Snow Range were identified as red deer-elk hybrids, escapees from a Colorado game farm. Colorado game farm ranchers themselves have reported that 231 elk and red deer have escaped into the wild.

The uproar that resulted was quickly calmed with the explanation that a few red deer genes in a handful of elk would not hybridize the entire America elk herd. But with the proliferation of game farms in western states in recent years,

Colonial settlers called the American elk a variety of names, while naturalists argued whether the European red deer and the American elk were biologically identical.

and their bent on bringing in exotic species, it certainly is cause for concern for any elk enthusiast who wants the Wapiti to remain a unique subspecies of Cervus elaphus.

The problem of red deer/elk hybridization dropped right into my lap this past spring. As acquisitions manager for Stoney-Wolf Video, a producer of outdoor videos, it was my job to study all incoming videos for possible inclusion into our line of videos.

I received a video from a New Zealand man, which contained a lot of wildlife footage, especially of red deer and Wapiti. As an elk lover and rabid student of the American elk, I was both mesmerized and bewildered by the array of various elk-like animals that paraded onto the screen. In the dark timbered mountains, I could not tell if an incoming animal was an elk or a red deer.

The only sure identifying method I had was the loud, guttural bellow of the red deer, as opposed to the hollow, musical bugle of the elk. By the time I was finished watching that video, I wasn't sure whether the animals I was viewing were red deer, Wapiti or hybrids.

Historically, elk probably entered the North American continent from Eurasia by way of the trans-Siberian land bridge between present day Russia and Alaska, which has periodically formed and been inundated through the ages.

When early colonists arrived in America, there were six subspecies of elk roaming this vast land. While there may be some disagreement, even among naturalists, about what constitutes a subspecies, the accepted qualifications are: physical difference and geographical isolation. As with any subspecies, there will be some intermingling where ranges overlap, but for the most part geographical isolation of various major elk herds through the ages had created six distinct and unique types of elk.

Eastern Elk

The Eastern elk was the animal that most colonists encountered when they set foot in the new world. The Eastern elk's vast range included all the eastern hardwood forests along the eastern seaboard and penetrated into the heart of the continent to the far edge of the great hardwood forests where the Great Plains began.

With scant natural grasses growing in the gloomy virgin hardwood forests, the Eastern elk depended almost exclusively on browse for its diet. However, early explorers noted that wherever small openings made by fire or flood allowed sun-nourished grass to flourish, the Eastern elk crowded into these places to greedily devour the grass.

Starving Pilgrims, and later westward-migrating Pioneers, decimated and eventually exterminated the Eastern elk. Biological information on this animal is scant and scientists have depended on historical accounts and skeletons to piece together the Eastern elk's physique.

The problem of red deer/elk hybridization is a real threat. Already, hundreds of red dee and hybrid elk have escaped from game farms.

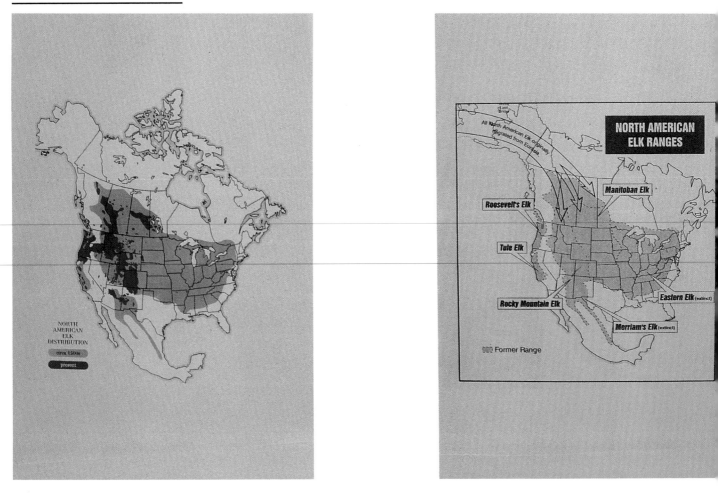

The historic distribution of elk versus today's elk herd graphically illustrates how much elk habitat has shrunk. Maps courtesy Rocky Mountain Elk Foundation.

Manitoban Elk

The Manitoban elk's range began where the eastern elk's range stopped — at the endless sea of grass on the Great Plains. The Manitoban elk is the species that Lewis & Clark wrote about as existing in vast herds scattered throughout the treeless prairie.

The Manitoban elk's range extended northward into Canada and westward to the foot of the Rocky Mountains. The Manitoban elk's southern range extended down into Texas until the grasslands were withered into cactus, sage, chaparral and desert.

Rocky Mountain Elk

The Rocky Mountain elk, sometimes referred to as the Yellowstone elk, roamed the rugged forests and mountains of the Rockies and associated mountain ranges westward into Washington and Oregon. Its northern range extended far into Canada and the Northwest Territories and southward along the southern Rockies until it melted into hot semi-desert habitat.

While it is generally believed that elk were driven into the mountains by the encroachment of civilization and commercial exploitation, many naturalists now believe that this species of mountain-loving elk always lived in the rugged isolation of the Rockies. This species probably found enough grass in the Rockies in areas where seasonal wildfires eliminated dark virgin forests, or where avalanche chutes wiped large sections of trees from mountain sides, and in natural grassy areas such as the Yellowstone ecosystem.

Roosevelt Elk

The Roosevelt elk inhabited, and still lives, in the mountains along the Pacific Coast. This is the largest of all American elk, with a mature bull often weighing over 1,000 pounds.

Roosevelt elk ranged through the dense forests and steep, brush-choked mountains of the Coastal Range. They are almost totally browsers, due to the infestations of dense alder, blackberry and mountain maple brush that grow under the dark canopy of huge coniferous trees.

Early explorers only caught fleeting glimpses of this secretive elk before it tunneled back into its rain forest jungles. And since most travelers tried hard to avoid the dense forests, the Roosevelt elk stayed secure and flourished in its dense, brush choked home range.

Merriam Elk

The Merriam elk lived in isolated mountain ranges in Mexico and northward into Arizona, Texas and New Mexico. By the time conservationists at the turn of the century attempted to save the Merriam elk from exploitation by cattle overgrazing and market hunting, this species was on the verge of extinction and slowly drifted into oblivion.

Very little is known about the physiology of the Merriam elk. Only a few antlers and skeletons remain to help scientists piece together the puzzle called the Merriam elk.

Tule Elk

The Tule elk ranged through the arid grasslands and marshy coastal country of western and northern California. This very specialized band of elk is the smallest species, with a mature bull weighing about 500 pounds.

Early explorers found the Tule elk to be very plentiful throughout this region, but exploitation by gold miners, fur trappers, and the development of their habitat for agriculture left only a small herd which tunneled back into the swampy coastal country.

Summary

Scientists estimate that upwards to 10 million elk roamed the North American Continent when the Pilgrims arrived. Vast herds of various subspecies of Wapiti roamed the land everywhere, providing food and clothing for all. In the beginning, it seemed like there would be an inexhaustible supply. In the end, there was not.

Both elk and Native Americans were migrants to North America through the ice bridge between Siberia and Alaska. Much of the Indian's life has been interwoven with the elk ever since.

Chapter Three

Indians and Elk

It is interesting to note that both Indians and elk were migrants to America. Archaeological evidence points to the ice bridge that appeared between Siberia and Alaska as the crossing point where Indians and elk gained access to North America about 12,000 years ago.

The Indian's life has been interwoven with the elk ever since. Though elk were not the major source of the Native Americans' sustenance, Indians pursued the elk throughout their free roaming history and valued it greatly.

Elk meat was used for food. Its hide was used for clothing, glue and tepee coverings. The elk's elongated, relatively light skeletal structure was prized for tools ranging from awls and scrapers to farming implements. Antlers were fashioned into ornaments, or spear and arrow points. And the elk tongue bundle was carried by the spiritual leader and contained "Big Medicine."

Elk teeth were prized as ornaments and were often used as a medium of barter or as money. These canine teeth, often referred to as whistlers, were true ivory tusks growing in the roof of an elk's mouth. Scientists believe that these tusks were once much longer, but through the process of evolution they became small and rounded. They are at a loss to even guess what these tusks had been used for in pre-historic elk.

One thing we know for sure. The Indians loved to see their women in dresses adorned with elk teeth. A favored woman might have upwards to 200 elk teeth sewed onto her dress and it signaled her status as a very special woman. Elk teeth were so hard to accumulate before the horse arrived, that tribes such as the Blackfeet did not even use elk teeth for jewelry because they were too hard to come by.

Before 1880, only women wore elk teeth. Among the Gros Ventre (Big Belly) Indians of Montana, elk teeth were considered the greatest of decorations — as long as a woman was wearing them. At a celebration near Fort Hays, a man showed up wearing a vest adorned with elk teeth and the Indians laughed at him, saying, "You crazy thing! Don't you know that only women wear elk teeth!" The man persisted and was eventually dismissed with a shake of the head and was considered "quite queer."

Before long, even the men began wearing the attractive elk teeth on their clothes. Indian women who were desperate to appear favored began cutting and

An Indian scout signals to a distant hunter waiting in ambush along a trail that an elk is coming. Hands held high above the head and waved back and forth was the universal Native American sign language for the Wapiti. Illustration by Dennis Althoff.

polishing antler tips to look like elk teeth and sewed them onto their dresses. A flourishing trade ensued with Pacific Coast tribes for small seashells, whose size and polished white luster closely resembled the coveted elk teeth.

All the major Indian tribes had their own language, and even sub-tribes could not easily communicate when they met on the prairie. However, certain hand signals were universal among the Native American cultures, and the symbol for the elk was one of them.

The Indian sign language for elk was to extend the fingers of both hands above the head pointing skyward, and then move the hands back and forth two or three times. Among hunting parties, a distant scout who appeared on the horizon and made this gesture instantly alerted his party that elk were ahead.

Generally, the Indian's way of life and his method of hunting can be separated into two eras — that period before the advent of the horse, and the years following its arrival. Indians throughout America were much more methodical and stationary before the horse arrived. They tended to be more of a hunter/gatherer/farmer society of people who were able to exist by adapting their lifestyle to suit the land.

As such, any hunting had to be done within a limited area which could be walked to, and back, within a reasonable period of time. Hunting was limited to the bow and arrow and other ingenious methods of killing animals for sustenance.

is Indian woman's dress is adorned with 200 elk teeth, which signified that she was
avored woman in the tribe.

Little is known about how the Indians hunted the elk east of the Mississippi because very few in-depth historical records were made of the Indians along the East Coast. By 1800 most of the elk east of the Mississippi had been killed by pioneers for food. Within a few decades, most of the free roaming Eastern Indians would follow the elk into oblivion.

However, many archaeological excavations of Indian sites throughout the eastern states have found elk bones and tools made from elk, and one site in Ohio unearthed an elk vertebra with a stone arrowhead imbedded in it. With the abundance of deer, small game and birds, and with the Eastern Indian's lack of horse power, it is doubtful that elk played a critical part in his daily hunts for food. The elk was probably sought more as a secondary source for its hide, bones, antlers and teeth because most archaeological sites usually found elk remains as tools or other useful implements.

Fortunately, a few historical accounts exist which relate how the Eastern Indian tribes, lacking horses and hunting mostly in dense cover, usually stalked or ambushed elk.

Ambush was the favorite hunting and fighting technique of the Eastern Indian tribes. In 1779, during General Sullivan's famous march from Pennsylvania to southern New York against the Iroquois Confederacy of Indian tribes, the

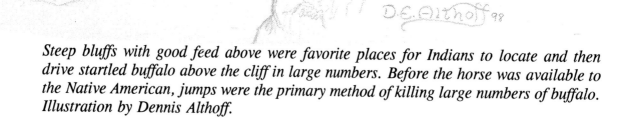

Steep bluffs with good feed above were favorite places for Indians to locate and then drive startled buffalo above the cliff in large numbers. Before the horse was available to the Native American, jumps were the primary method of killing large numbers of buffalo. Illustration by Dennis Althoff.

militia was constantly harassed by Indians who, dressed in buckskin, would kneel in the brush along the trail and then bend forward while facing away from the oncoming troops. The approaching militia often walked right by these stump-like Indians before the natives suddenly jumped up, flung a few arrows, and then disappeared into the dense forest.

No doubt, the Eastern elk was hunted in the same manner, especially in the steep Appalachian and Blue Ridge Mountains where game trails were heavily used

Snares were used extensively by Indians, especially in heavily forested terrain where the elk used trails. This Indian waits with snare ready along a heavily used game trail for a cow elk driven from the prairie by other Indians. Illustration by Dennis Althoff.

by both elk and Indians.

From the accounts of early explorers, historians and archaeologists, Indian life and elk hunting methods west of the Mississippi have been extensively documented, and several ingenious hunting methods have emerged. They range from simple snares and pits, to complicated jumps and surrounds.

Jumps

Elk hunting in the more open terrain west of the Mississippi was difficult, and elk were seldom killed, en masse, except at specific locations, such as jumps. A jump site usually consisted of a cliff or very steep embankment, with a good feeding area above. The Indians kept casual track of these jump sites, and when a herd of buffalo or elk wandered onto the plain above the jump site, a hasty hunt was planned.

The younger men and youths who could run fast, covered themselves with animal skins and then wandered, bent over, into the open. Slowly, these men flanked both sides of the herd so they could not run to the side of the jump when alerted. A string of men then carefully positioned themselves on a line on the far side of the animals.

When everyone was in position, a signal was given, and the Indians threw off their disguises. The startled animals ran hysterically away from the Indians who chased them, toward the jump. Their speed of flight, and the Indians' loud yelling behind them, usually sent the fleeing animals over the edge en masse. Women and older men waited below to kill the crippled animals and butcher the carcasses.

While this was a favorite method of pre-horse Indians to kill buffalo in great numbers, elk were also slaughtered at these jumps. Early explorers tell of finding jump areas where the ground below was littered with huge piles of bleached elk and buffalo bones from hundreds of years of use.

In 1832, Warren Angus Ferris, a member of a trapping party near Green River, Wyoming, told of navigating a steep trail along a precipice caused by the scouring of the river below. He noted that at the foot of the bluff were the bones of many buffalo and elk that had been run off the cliff and killed.

While most of the major jump areas were ravaged by commercial bone pickers (used for fertilizer) and theft from souvenir hunters, it was not that long ago when a traveler could still find lesser known jump areas with skeletons still intact. Lloyd Paul, a Chippewa-Cree friend of mine, told me that as a boy on the Rocky Boy Indian Reservation of North-Central Montana, he often scrounged through several old jump sites for arrowheads and recalls finding several stone heads imbedded in bones. Today, these sites have been picked clean.

Roundups

Roundups, often referred to as corrals or surrounds, were used to capture and kill large numbers of animals, elk included. The Indians usually had several areas, much like the jumps, that they checked frequently to see if any animals were in a feeding area where they could be carefully driven into a blind canyon or river, where waiting Indians would surround the milling herd and shoot arrows into them.

Indians also adapted the roundup to be a portable hunting method. When a herd of grazing elk was spotted, some tribes built corrals of rocks, brush or logs nearby, but out of sight of the herd. Men with skins covering them meandered into the open, and when they were in the proper position, they threw off the hides and charged the herd, yelling loudly and waving their arms. The startled animals, if the plan was well-laid, ran away from them and into the corral, where the confused, milling animals were shot by Indians lying in wait.

Snares

Snares were used extensively by Indians, especially in the forested and mountainous terrain where game was often forced to use a specific trail to navigate

The introduction of the horse changed the Indian culture forever. Now, the horse mounted hunter could chase and kill elusive large animals such as the buffalo and elk. Photo courtesy Montana Historical Society.

the steep sidehills or streams. Snaring was especially popular among the Pacific Coast tribes, and these Indians devised two different elk snaring methods.

The first method used a simple twisted sinew or hemp rope hung over a trail where fresh elk tracks had been found. The trail was then funneled to a width that would barely allow the elk to pass through. The snare was lowered down from a stout tree to the level of the elk's head. These snares were checked daily and any animal caught was usually shot with arrows until it died.

Unfortunately, many things could go wrong with this unmanned snare. An elk might decide to duck under the loop, or a bull's antlers might be too wide to slip into the snare loop. But more often than not, a failed snare setup was the result of an elk getting caught, and then using its huge size and power to eventually break the snare.

For that reason, Indians often chose to use springpole snares. A stout fir tree sapling was bent over and secured by a cord. Attached to the sapling was a strong noose suspended at head height above the trail. A jerk of the noose released the trigger, and the rope tightened around the animal's neck, but the resilience of the fir prevented the elk from exerting its full force against the snare rope. Eventually, the animal would become exhausted and lie down.

Another common, but effective, snare was a large-meshed sinew net stretched between two resilient fir trees across a game trail. At each end, a hunter or two lay in wait, while others drove the quarry into the snare. In this manner, not only elk, but also deer and bear were captured.

In more open terrain, Indians often hunted elk by having several men slip into dense cover near where the elk were feeding in the open. These men then climbed trees above the main game trails. Each hunter tied a very stout rope to the tree and then made a large noose at the other end.

Other men then walked into the open, causing the elk to run for the nearby cover. When an elk ran along the trail, the hunter would lower his snare and catch the fleeing animal. The benefit of this method was that the man in the tree could adjust the height of the snare loop to accommodate an elk running with its head up or down. Also, the hunter was right there when the elk was caught, so he could kill it quickly with a few well-placed arrows before it broke the rope.

Dogs

Dogs were very useful to the pre-horse Indian, not only for carrying his belongings during his frequent moves, but also for hunting. The Pacific Coast Salish tribes used dogs extensively to root out elk from the impenetrable brush jungles of the coastal rain forests.

The hunters of the Wiyot Tribe of Oregon performed a curious rite before taking up the hunt with dogs. In preparation for an elk hunt, a man lived apart from his wife for as long as two months, but did not abstain from food.

Then he went out with his medium sized "coyote dogs" often numbering two or more. Upon finding elk tracks, sometimes a day or two old, he set the dogs on them. Often times, it took days to run down the elk. During that time, the hunter ate nothing, but he did smoke.

When the dogs finally had the exhausted elk at bay, the hunter shot it. After cutting up and hanging the carcass, the hunter returned to the village and a group was sent out to retrieve it. The meat was divided equally among these people, and the remainder was smoked. This kind of hunting was called, "Raqhli," which means a pack of wolves chasing an elk.

These coastal tribes also used dogs to solve their problem with having the elk break their snares. They often set snares with the end of the rope tied to a small log. When the elk was snared, it easily ran off, but with the log dragging behind. When a snare was found missing, a hunter with dogs was sent to track the elk. The combination of yapping dogs at its heels, and the strain of the log constantly tangled in the brush, usually brought the elk to bay quickly, and it was shot by the hunter.

Pits

Pits were a common elk hunting device among Indians throughout elk country, but especially in those areas where the elk were more likely to follow established trails, such as along streams or in mountains. Unfortunately, the Indians often could not dig a pit deep enough to keep a long-legged elk from jumping back out. To keep the elk in the pit, sharpened stakes were rammed into the bottom of the pit to impale the elk and keep it from jumping out. And even if it did escape, the belly wounds from the stakes usually forced it to lie down and die nearby.

Great care was taken at these pits to lay a thin mat over the opening and then cover it with natural grasses and moss, so that the finished surface could not easily be detected as false. Surely, the local Indians knew where these deadly pits were located and easily avoided them, but many a stranger must have fallen into these deadly traps.

The simplicity and effectiveness of the pit for taking elk caused some Indian tribes to rely on it solely for their elk needs. The Achomawi Indians of Northern California had so many elk pits dug in game trails along one particularly good elk hunting river, that the river became known as the Pit River, and the Indians were referred to as the Pit River Indian Tribe.

Deep Snow

In northern climates, Indians also found good hunting for elk during winter by roaming through the deep snow on snowshoes and then running down elk floundering in the deep snow. When conditions were just right, Indians often slaughtered many elk on one hunt when the snow depth was too much for the struggling animals to escape.

The Horse Mounted Indian Hunter

The introduction of the horse to Indian culture changed it forever. Since their arrival in America in 1532, the Spanish forbade Indians to own horses or guns. But in the 1600's Apache raids on Spanish outposts in the Southwest finally wrestled the horse into Indian hands. A flourishing trade system that already existed between Indian tribes of the Southwest and Northern Plains Indians soon brought the horse to a native people who had for millennia wistfully watched with grumbling bellies as great hordes of deer, elk and buffalo safely roamed just out of range over the open Plains.

But with a horse under him, an Indian could charge right into the midst of these great herds and kill more than enough animals to feed his tribe. It so irrevocably changed the Indian way of life that many Plains tribes refused to hunt on foot.

And who could blame them! With 40 million buffalo and nine million elk roaming the Plains, there was no need to expend any effort to hunt deer or elk the old way. It got so bad among some tribes that the braves just about refused to get off their horses to do anything except sleep and eat.

Unfortunately, the buffalo was not always readily available. The great roaming herds often disappeared during the night, with the trail leading far off into another hostile tribe's territory. That often forced the horse mounted Indian to turn to the elk for sustenance.

But even on horseback, the Indian did not have an easy time hunting elk. Unlike the buffalo, which was relatively slow and lumbering, and could be stampeded en masse and then shot by horse-mounted hunters, the elk were much faster and tended to scatter toward thickets and mountains where horse pursuit became difficult and dangerous for both horse and rider. Many Indian tribes, such as the Chippewa and Sarci, considered their horses too valuable a commodity to risk losing one in a break-neck charge across the prairie after the fleet-footed elk.

Other tribes, such as the Blackfeet, Comanche, Crow and Sioux, adapted their horse hunting techniques to suit plains elk hunting. Rather than charging an elk herd, these Indians often broke up into small units and circled the herd. One small group then rode into the open and flushed the elk, which usually ran for cover. In that cover, dismounted hunters lay in wait along game trails and ambushed passing elk. Other horse mounted hunters cut off the fleeing elk and shot arrows into them as they ran by.

Occasionally, the absence of buffalo regulated the elk to extremely important status. One account relates how a war party of Absarokee Indians that was returning from a raid on the Nez Perce in Idaho, ran dangerously short of meat on their return trip to Montana.

They returned along the Bighorn River, prime buffalo country, but the Shoshone had been hunting there recently, and there were no buffalo. Desperate for food, they turned their full attention to elk. A scout was sent out and located a large herd of elk. He reported back to the chief, and they all started out to hunt the elk. Each man had a slow and a fast horse with him.

Crossing to the southwest, they split into two bands, and one on each side chased the elk like they did with buffalo down to a low muddy area where the elk could not run fast. The Indians then switched to their fresh, faster horses, and they killed many elk that day.

Not all Indian hunters were so fortunate. Thomas Jefferson Farnam, a white explorer traveling with Comanche Indians along the Arkansas River in 1838, wrote, "We are fatigued and famished, and every member of the party is stretched within himself. Twice, we spotted elk, and horse mounted hunters slipped into ravines and advanced toward the elk, while other hunters exposed their position so that the elk would not notice the approaching hunters. This worked very well, and the men were able to get within 300 yards of the watching elk before the men burst out of the ravine and galloped after the elk.

"Never did horses run nearest their topmost speed for a stake in dollars than ours did for a steak of meat. But alas! The little advantage gained at the start, from the bewildered inaction of the game, began to diminish as soon as these fleet coursers of the prairie laid their nimble hoofs to the sward and pledged life upon speed.

"A few balls were sent whistling after them, but they soon slept in the earth, instead of the panting hearts they were designed to render pulseless; we returned to our lonely and hungry march."

The Indian Bow & Arrows

The Indian preferred the bow to harvest game even as big as elk and buffalo. Even when single shot flintlocks became available from hide and fur traders, the Indian still preferred a bow and a fistful of arrows for hunting instead of the cumbersome, loud, single shot rifle. A horse-mounted Indian could send flying from just about any riding position five of these lethal shafts in the time it took an experienced woodsman to reload his single shot flintlock.

efore the gun, Indians used sharpened stone, such as this flint knife, and obsidian or
ate arrowheads to kill elk and buffalo.

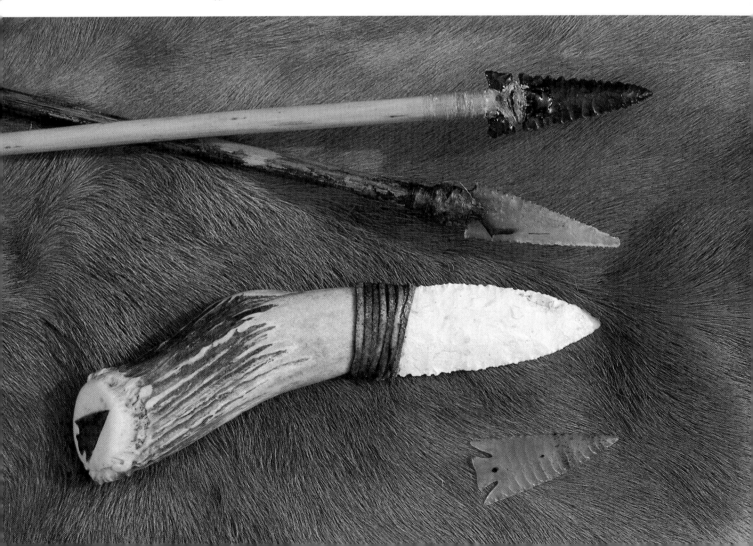

While it is true that the Indian was eventually defeated by armed U. S. Cavalry in later years when long range repeating rifles were invented, the outcome of a confrontation between swarming Indians and white men armed with single shot flintlocks often went to the Indian, because of his breakneck riding ability with arrows whizzing constantly at the enemy from every conceivable position, including from under the horse's belly.

Most Indian bows were made of wood, with sinew backing for strength and longevity because a plain wood bow tended to lose its strength after a short period of use.

The strongest bows were made from sheep or elk horns. The horn was boiled, straightened, worked into bow shape, and then spliced to obtain the necessary length of about three and a half feet. Threads of sinew from the neck and shoulder of buffalo were stretched on a flat piece of wood the width of the bow, and when this band was dry it was carefully taken from its temporary support and placed on the ground in order to moisten it and give it pliancy. This backing was then carefully fastened onto the bow with strong glue, made by boiling the neck skin of an elk, membrane from beaver tails, tips of elk horn, and

Young Indian boys like this one had bow in hand soon after they were walking. By the time they were ready to hunt, they were deadl shots. Photo courtesy Montana Historical Society.

hide scrapings. These bows kept their temper indefinitely.

Arrow shafts were usually made of any stout, straight-limbed bush or reed, such as willow or viburnum. Arrowheads were chipped from the best native stone that would nap well and take a good edge. The favorite arrowhead material came from flint or the family of glass-like rock called chalcedony, of which the favorite was black obsidian. These heads chipped into finely-napped points that took a razor's edge. Obsidian became a major trade item, and arrowheads made from this material appeared among tribes many hundreds of miles from the major obsidian mines of Montana.

Historians have given us a peek into the reasons why Indians were so adept with the relatively crude bow and arrow. One early-day visitor at an Assiniboine camp in Canada noted that youth starting at the age of four up through eighteen years spent nearly half their time shooting arrows at targets. Normal marksmanship among Indians was to hit a two inch target at thirty to forty yards.

When not fighting with other tribes or hunting elk and buffalo, warriors often played horseback games of skill during which the rider would shoot at targets while charging by on his horse.

Still, the stone-tipped arrow shot from an Indian bow was designed more for short range shooting, or at thinner skinned game such as deer. A horse mounted Indian hunter usually rode alongside a fleeing buffalo and then tried to ram an arrow down between its ribs, or send a shaft quartering forward after it entered the buffalo behind the ribcage.

Beyond point-blank range, the thick hide and massive bone structure of the buffalo, and to a lesser extent, the elk, caused penetration problems for the Indian. While on their epic journey, Lewis & Clark recorded several instances when they shot elk and discovered arrowheads imbedded only a short distance into the animal and covered with gristle.

In fact, some tribes, such as the Pacific Coast Salish tribes, aimed for the belly of the animal where the hide was thinner and no large bones would stop penetration. Being excellent trackers, these Indians then allowed the gut-shot elk to trot off and lie down. Within a few hours, peritonitis (contamination of the body cavity with bacteria from the paunch) made the animal too sick to flee, and the Indian then moved in and finished off the wounded elk.

The Indian and the Gun

As previously mentioned, the horse allowed the Indian to become mobile and follow the great game herds of the Plains. The Indian's procurement of the gun in the early 1800's, at first, had little impact because these early muzzleloading trade guns tended to be crude firearms whose accuracy was questionable even at a close range.

But by 1860, high powered single-shot Sharps rifles, and then long range repeating Henry rifles, became available to the Indian. Now, he could sit on a bluff 300 yards away and drop an elk in its tracks without having to chase the fleet-footed beast across the prairie.

This combination of horse and long range repeating rifle suddenly allowed the Indian to kill much more than he needed to sustain a harmonious existence on the Plains. The Indian's life suddenly improved, and for the first time he had a surplus to barter with white traders. It is ironic that these two improvements to Indian life, the horse and the gun, would also lead to his swift demise.

Common Indian Names For Elk

While the Northern Shoshonean term of "Wapiti" is the most common Native American name used for the elk, it must be remembered that there were many different Indian tribes with their own languages, and the name "elk" was pronounced differently among each tribe. Below are a few of the names given to the elk by various Indian tribes.

Plateau (Southern) Shoshonean	Pa-ru-hi'-ya
Piegan (Blackfoot)	Pun-nu-ka'
Cheyenne	Mo'-e
Flathead	Ts'he-tse
Nez Perce	We-wo'-ki-u
Cree	Wa-wa's-ke-siu
Sarsi	Tsu'z-zi
Northern Assiniboine	He-ha'-ga
Crow	Its'i-rikya'-ce
Dakota Sioux	Heli'aka
Kalispel	Ts'he-tsu
Washo	Han-ak-mu'-we'-u
Spokane	Ts'hets
Zuni	Tsai'-lu-sa

Chapter Four

The Elk Holocaust

The game herds that roamed America when the Pilgrims arrived staggered the imagination. Some naturalists estimated that sixty million buffalo and ten million elk co-existed with about two million Native Americans when the first European settlers came ashore at Plymouth Rock.

That number dwindled appreciably through the rapid expansion of the colonies to the banks of the Mississippi. By 1800 most of the bison and elk had been eliminated from the eastern forests by starving pioneers and settlers. However, there were still an estimated forty million buffalo and about nine million elk in the vast lands west of the Mississippi in the early 1800's, and no one at that time would have guessed that by the latter part of the century, both of these great animals would be virtually exterminated.

It is almost impossible to relate the slaughter of the great elk herds without first examining the events leading up to the demise of the buffalo because both species co-existed within the same habitat. And yet both of these animals' demise was inextricably tied to the beaver fur trade. As such, all three tragic chapters in the natural history of America are irrevocably interwoven as one massive, ignorant exploitation of America's resources.

The Beaver Fur Trade

Colonial and European manufacturers had always liked the fur of the beaver because it was dense and soft, yet it could be sheared to any length and then dyed to the desired color. The major problem was the dwindling supply of beaver pelts because the eastern streams had been trapped out by 1800.

That all changed when early explorers who had ventured into the unsettled lands west of the Mississippi returned with stories of vast colonies of beavers residing in just about every river and stream. This news created a brisk demand for beaver fur garments, especially sheared and dyed beaver fur hats.

Early day trappers and competing fur companies from the United States and Canada found bountiful trapping in 1816, when the fur boom began in earnest. But in those early days, much of the unexplored West was still firmly controlled by Indians, and many a trapper who had pelted beavers, eventually had his scalp pelted by hostile Indians and sold to British fur companies, who paid a bounty on American trappers' scalps, as an incentive to the Indians to keep American trappers out of the virgin beaver trapping areas they wanted for themselves.

The elk holocaust was the last of the massive wildlife exploitations in frontier America, following the beaver and buffalo slaughters. Photo courtesy National Park Service.

...e beaver was plentiful in most streams west of the Mississippi ...d spawned the great Mountain Man trapping movement in the ...rly 1800's.

Though the era of the fur trapping mountain man is still one of the highlights of the spirit of adventure in American history, it lasted barely more than a decade. The beaver is an easy animal to trap, and what was once thought to be an inexhaustible resource was becoming increasingly difficult to find by 1830. As more white trappers encroached upon Indian territory seeking beaver, the inevitable conflicts arose, and the U.S. Cavalry was used to subdue the hostiles, as the term went. This meant a series of forts and outposts were built deep into the heart of unknown Indian country to protect white adventurers and early settlers who ventured into this land that was claimed, and often treatied, by the red man.

By 1834, with beaver harvests declining, the furriers back East were also becoming bored with the beaver, and the silk top hat began to supplant the beaver fur in fashion circles. Trapping harvests began to decline after that. Though the fur trade continued for about another decade, beaver pelts sold for only half of what they had ten years before.

It was during the latter stages of the fur trapping era that the stage was set for the unprecedented animal holocaust that was to ensue over the next few decades, as travelers returned to civilization with stories of vast herds of elk and buffalo.

Buffalo: Annihilation Of An Endless Resource

The decline of the fur trade left thousands of mountain men stranded in the great expanse of prairie and mountain looking for something to do. These were men grown accustomed to total freedom, some called it reckless abandon, to do whatever they wanted. The thought of self-control or respect for another race's

By 1834, beaver harvests were declining and the fur was out of fashion, so tanners turned to the buffalo and elk, setting the stage for an unprecedented wildlife holocaust.

culture or livelihood was unheard of in that generation.

At first, it appeared that the supply of the buffalo was endless. One young trapper who had just ridden into St. Louis related, "Ever since I dropped off the east side of the Rockies, there has not been a moment when I could not look out and see vast herds of buffalo and elk. Not until I got here to the doorstep of civilization did the herds thin out." Even the naturalists fell victim to the illusion. Paleontologist O. C. Marsh found buffalo so abundant in Kansas that the possibility of their extinction did not seriously occur to him.

It's easy to visualize back then how a spectator to a great passing buffalo herd could be awed into complacency, because many of the largest herds simply exceeded the power of the eye to appraise their enormity. For instance, witnesses near present day Regina, Saskatchewan, reported a herd on the move which stretched in each direction as far as one could see and, counted at several hundred per minute, required twenty-four hours to pass. They estimated its number at 1,000,000!

When the buffalo harvest began, many new and unforeseen problems arose. The logistics of transporting buffalo hides back East was staggering. Whereas, a bale of 100 beaver pelts weighing a hundred and fifty pounds had fetched $500 in St. Louis — that same weight totaled only ten buffalo hides and brought just $70. This problem was solved by using large barges and steamships to carry hides down the major tributaries to the Mississippi and on to St. Louis.

But the biggest problem was the actual pursuit of the buffalo. There simply were not enough white men to get the job done. In fact, during the peak of the buffalo slaughter, only about 100,000 of the 2,000,000 hides marketed annually were attributed to white hunters. In an ironic and tragic scenario, the traders turned to the residents of buffalo country, the Indian, to satiate the great demand for hides.

The forts that had been built to protect early settlers and travelers from hostile Indians now became major hubs for commercial hide traffic. Trading outposts also sprang up in isolated areas where trade with the Indians was most lucrative.

For the Indian's part, he was a relatively simplistic dweller of the prairie and mountains who had for centuries lived a compatible life among these great herds. Meat was the staple food, along with roots and berries, and tools were crude bone and hide implements. So when a trader offered the average Indian even the most basic items for trade, such as beads or a knife, he reacted with childlike wonderment and glee. Indeed, a utensil as simple as a needle awl (much easier to use than the laborious Indian bone awl) might cost an Indian five beaver pelts, which brought $30 in St. Louis.

Below is a listing of the posted rates for trade with Indians at an American Fur Trading Post in 1834:

1 Beaver or Robe	1 common blanket
1 Beaver or Robe	1 shirt
1 Beaver or Robe	1/2 yard blue cloth
1 Beaver or Robe	1/2 yard scarlet cloth
12 beavers or Robes	1 rifle
1 Elk Skin	1 bunch common cut beads
1 Elk Skin	30 loads ammo
1 Elk Skin	20 loads ammo & 1 knife
1 Elk Skin	20 loads ammo & small bunch beads
1 Elk Skin	20 loads ammo & 1/2 doz small buttons
1 Elk Skin	20 loads ammo & small tobacco

In the past, Indians had very little surplus to trade for even the most mundane items, but with the arrival of the horse, and then the long range repeating rifle, things changed quickly — and irrevocably. This combination of horse and long range rifle suddenly allowed the Indian to kill much more than he needed to sustain a harmonious existence. A good example was found with the Flathead Indians of Western Montana, who were known for their fearlessness in battle, but friendliness towards whites. They had once been a people of peaceful nature who had reverence for the land and the animals, but the allure of whisky and cheap trade trinkets was too much even for this especially proud native people.

John Fahey wrote in his book, *The Flathead Indians*: "The successful Flathead hunter who once prized his hard-won robe and his tepee of twelve or twenty-four hides now collected more skins than he could use. He killed wantonly and discarded less desirable buffalo products. In this way, the horse contributed to the destruction of the bison. The Flathead man, needing additional women in his lodge to clean and tan the growing accumulation of hides, often took several wives. To please a favored one, a Flathead hunter might trade a horse for sixty or seventy elk's teeth to decorate a dress for her."

By 1850, the once endless herd possibly totalling sixty million buffalo had been reduced to twenty million. About 200,000 hides were being marketed annually, but observers noted that less than a third of the buffalo killed actually

At first, the supply of buffalo seemed endless. Waste was common, and it was estimated that only one hide from five slaughtered buffalo ever made it to market. Photo courtesy Montana Historical Society.

were skinned, and half of those were kept for local use. The resulting estimate was that upwards to three million buffalo were being slaughtered annually in every conceivable manner by both Indian and white.

Tales of bravado and conquest were common in that period, with little consideration given to the fact that these were living, breathing animals that were being killed by the millions. (No doubt because the buffalo was considered to be a dim-witted, lumbering, unattractive animal.) For instance, William (Buffalo Bill) Cody once had a contest with a fellow hunter to see who could kill the most buffalo in a single day. Cody won. He killed sixty-nine, while his competitor killed "only" forty-six. Cody estimated that in one eighteen-month period, he'd killed 4,280 buffalo.

Slowly, the lives of the once-proud Native American people of the Plains were being reduced to the level of indentured servants to the hide market. In one small Montana outpost called Fort McKenzie along the Missouri River, the once-feared Blackfeet Indians had become literally addicted to the lifeline of the trader's wares and annually brought upwards to 25,000 hides for trade.

So tied had the Blackfeet become to this trading narcotic, that they usually set up their camps right outside the fort. This splendid tribe of fierce, magnificent warriors who were once the scourge of the Plains, was typical of almost all the other Indian Peoples who's lifestyles had been reduced to the mindless slaughter of their life-sustaining food source. Slain buffalo were hastily skinned and left to rot on the prairie while the hunters quickly returned to the trading post to turn in their hides for tobacco, sugar or whiskey.

By the winter of 1882-83, only about 75,000 buffalo existed north of the Yellowstone River in Montana Territory. Fear and instinct drove the herd northward toward the Canadian border. No one knows if it was the professional market hunters, or the half-starved Cree and Blackfoot Indians who were responsible, but by spring only a few hundred were found scattered in ravines along the Musselshell River. The rest of that last big herd had simply ceased to exist.

By the spring of 1883, a herd of about 10,000 head was discovered ranging near the Black Hills of North Dakota. Market hunters speedily killed almost 9,000 of them. In the fall of that year the hunters finally located the remaining thousand buffalo. But about that time, Sitting Bull and a thousand of his warriors arrived on the scene. The white and red man joined forces in one final wildlife orgy, and within two days the entire herd had been annihilated.

But news travelled slowly in those days. The buffalo butchers, as usual, outfitted themselves with wagon loads of supplies and ammunition and set out for the buffalo range. They searched far and wide, but the only buffalo sign they found was the putrefied carrion from previous hunts. The buffalo hunters were astounded that the buffalo could be gone, and they staggered back home in failure and, ultimately, bankruptcy.

The final chapter was written in the spring of 1884 when a robe buyer was able to collect barely enough robes to fill one train car. That was the last shipment of buffalo robes sent back East on the Northern Pacific Railroad.

The free roaming buffalo was gone — forever. And what of the Indian? The story goes that a few years later a white man saw a band of Indians riding as in days of old toward buffalo country in silence and sadness.

The white man asked, "Where are you bound?"

The Indians answered, "For the buffalo."

"But there are no more."

"No, we know it."

"Then why are you going on such a foolish chase?" The white man asked.

The Indian replied, "Because we always go at this time."

While dreadful historical accounts of massacres during the Indian Wars remain a modern focal point of the Indian's demise, violent death in war was but a minor dent in the crash of the great Native American Peoples. Historians unanimously agree that it was the exploitation and elimination of the buffalo that effectively doomed the free roaming Indian civilizations to starvation, disease and cultural oblivion.

The Elk Holocaust

Toward the end, buffalo hides were beginning to fall out of favor with tanners in favor of elk hides. At that time, a buffalo hide was bringing about $3.50, while an elk hide fetched about $7.50. Considering the fact that the average American's annual salary at that time was about $170 per year, it didn't take much prodding or soul-searching by those in the hide trade to turn their full fury against the hapless elk.

The combination of long range rifles and improved transportation systems, such as the newly completed transcontinental railroad into the heart of the West, greatly aided market hunters seeking those secluded areas that had been passed over in prior years for the more easily obtained buffalo.

And just like the buffalo slaughter, the greatest by-product of the elk holocaust was waste. It was estimated that for every buffalo hide that made it to market, five were killed and wasted. Considering the facts that the same hunting methods, transportation problems, and market hunters were at work with the elk, it is probable that only one in five elk that were killed made it to the hide market.

But worse than that, only about one percent of the edible meat of the elk was ever used. During one winter hunt in northeast Wyoming in 1870, more than 4,000 elk were slaughtered by market hunters. The only parts saved were some of the hides and the tongues.

By the 1880's massive encroachment of civilization on historical elk range by ranchers and settlers also added to the elk's woes. By 1890, the elk had literally nowhere to hide on the prairie. The great herds' existence was dependent upon wintering in lowlands at the foot of the mountains where snow depth was usually moderate.

It was there that hungry whites and Indians awaited the ill-fated elk migrations with massive firepower. An early day sport hunter named G.O. Shields lamented the berserk slaughter of his beloved elk when he wrote, "Here the market hunter can find a ready market for the meats and skins he brings in, and an opportunity to spend the proceeds of such outrageous traffic on ranch whiskey and revelry.

"The ranchmen themselves hunt and lay down a stock of meat for the year when the game comes down into the valleys. The Indians, when they have eaten up their allotment of Government rations, lie in wait for the elk in the same manner. So that when the great snows of autumn or winter fall in the high ranges, when the elk band together and seek refuge in the valleys, they find a mixed and hungry horde waiting for them at the mouth of every canyon. Before they have reached the valley where the snowfall is light enough to allow them to live through the winter, their skins are drying in the neighboring shacks."

President Theodore Roosevelt, himself an avid sportsman who had a keen affection for the stately beauty of the elk, also mentioned with alarm their disappearance from his ranch in Montana. He stated in his memoirs, "I have occasionally killed elk in the neighborhood of my ranch on the little Missouri. They were very plentiful along this river until 1881, but the last of the big bands were slaughtered or scattered about that time. Smaller bunches were found for two or three years longer, and to this day, scattered individuals linger here and there in the most remote and inaccessible parts of the broken country.

"In old times they were often found on the open prairie, and were fond of sunning themselves on the sand bars by the river, even at midday, while they often fed by daylight. Nowadays the few survivors dwell in the timber of the most remote ravines, and only venture out at even or nightfall. Thanks to their wariness

a macabre twist of fate, many of those hide hunters who had wantonly butchered and ...asted the buffalo for many years, were themselves starving after the buffalo was gone ...nd resorted to picking bones to eke out a living. Photo courtesy Montana Historical ...ociety.

Only one percent of the slaughtered elk meat was used, and many of the hides were also left to rot by gluttonous hide hunters. By the 1880's some naturalists considered the elk all but extinct due to massive market hunting. Photo courtesy National Park Service.

and seclusiveness, their presence is often not even noticed by cowboys or others who ride through their haunts; and so the hunters only know vaguely of their existence. It thus happens that the last individuals of species may linger in a locality for many years after the rest of their kind have vanished; on the Little Missouri today every elk (as in the Rockies every buffalo) killed is at once set down as 'the last of its race'."

G.O. Shields echoed these sentiments when he wrote, "It is sad to think that such a noble creature as the American elk is doomed to early and absolute extinction, but such is nevertheless the fact. Year by year his mountain habitat is being surrounded and encroached upon by the advancing lines of settlements. These lines are the ranches of cattle and sheep growers, the cabins and towns of miners, the stations and residences of employees of the railroads."

By the late 1880's, some naturalists already considered the elk all but extinct, with death being the inevitable fate of those few elk who had somehow eluded the bullet or bow thus far. In acts often bordering on macabre bravado, those few miserable buffalo or elk that were flushed out of some isolated pocket were mercilessly hunted by glory seeking gunmen, with the result being the actual extermination of that species in a particular valley, county or state.

Though these facts reveal the senseless butchery and insensitivity of an ignorant people gorging on, and abusing, the bounty of the land, there is actually a silver lining behind this dark cloud. The outcry of concerned, influential individuals toward the end of this holocaust also gave birth to one of the most concentrated and influential conservation movements in the world, but it didn't come easy.

Chapter Five

A Rough Rider Saves The Elk
(Teddy Roosevelt To The Rescue)

One of the few places where a small herd of elk had survived the market hunters was located in a remote, rugged area of northwestern Wyoming called Colter's Hell. Colter was a mountain man who had returned from an exploration of the area with wild-eyed tales of a surreal land where giant cauldrons bubbled and geysers spouted year around; where elk and buffalo, and other wildlife still existed in an area of yellowish sandstone. His fellow mountain men were understandably skeptical of his description of this strange place and jokingly quipped that it sounded like Colter had discovered hell! The Indians knew about this land of wonder and had a name for it. They called it the land of the yellow stone.

After several scientific expeditions into the area, the Yellowstone Protection Act was created by Congress in 1872, which officially protected the land and its inhabitants. The only problem was that nothing specific had been entered into law to protect the elk, and with no money having been allotted for a budget, the Park lay at the mercy of exploiters. At that time, Yellowstone was a remote, isolated corner of the West where very few travelers passed through, and it had no permanent residents. But word quickly got around about the natural wonders of Yellowstone, and increasing numbers of early day tourists began visiting the Park.

Roads were built and people moved in, with the inevitable results. The isolated elk herd that had only a few years before numbered about 400 animals, had increased to 7,000. But greed reared its ugly head again. Poaching and market hunting began in earnest in the Park, right under the noses of those few timid and outmanned caretakers. One chagrined observer wrote, "The game in the Park had been shot with impunity and marketed at the hotels without any interference on the part of the officers whose sworn duty it was to protect and prevent its destruction."

The major problem wasn't that the market hunters were slaughtering vast herds of elk. That was not possible. There were no more vast herds! Tragic reports of wholesale elk slaughter continued in the early years of the Park. In 1875 Park representative, General William Strong wrote, "When the snow falls and fierce winter storms begin in November and December, the elk, deer and sheep leave the summits of the snowy ranges and come in great bands to the foot-hills and valleys of the Park, where they are met and shot down shamefully by those merciless human vultures."

No one locally seemed able or willing to even attempt to physically stop these market hunters who were armed to the teeth. Representative Ludlow wrote a year later, "Hunters have for years devoted themselves to the slaughter of the game, until within the limits of the Park it is hardly to be found. I was credibly informed by people on the spot, and personally cognizant of the facts, that during the winter of 1874 and 1875, at which season the snows render the elk an easy prey, no less than 1,500 to 2,000 of these, the largest and finest game animals in the country, were thus destroyed within the fifteen mile radius of Mammoth Springs. From this large number, representing an immense supply of the best food, the skins only were taken, netting the hunter some $2.50 apiece, the frozen carcasses being left in the snow to feed wolves or decay in the spring."

Due to this sustained loss of wildlife to poachers, a frustrated Ludlow made a recommendation that would eventually bring into play the one force that could stand up to the murderous poachers. Ludlow made a personal appeal to the Secretary of the Interior recommending that the U.S. Cavalry be stationed in the Park to provide protection from vandals and the impudent poachers.

But the U.S. Cavalry did not immediately come to the rescue with trumpet blaring. More impassioned pleas were sent to the Secretary of the Interior in Washington. This message from Park Superintendent Norris in 1877 stated, in emphatic terms, that the Park's wildlife had been decimated. "The unquestioned facts are that over 2,000 hides of the huge Rocky Mountain elk, nearly as many big horn, deer and antelope, and scores if not hundreds of moose and bison were taken out of the Park in spring of 1875, and probably 7,000 since its discovery in 1870. These animals are often run down on showshoes and tomahawked when their carcasses were least valuable."

On a hot, muggy day in August of 1886 a bedraggled line of troops finally arrived to "save" Yellowstone. Surely, the first impression by the resident poachers who watched Captain Moses Harris and his motley looking M Troop dismount and report for duty, was a smirk. The smirk faded quickly.

These were men who took the job of protecting the last elk herd seriously. They had the law of the U.S. Government on their side. They also had toughness and firepower on their side — and they weren't afraid to use it to whatever degree was necessary to get the job done.

Apprehended poachers were made to pay, in more ways than one. An outlaw who was caught hide hunting at the southern end of the Park was immediately banished, but not to a casual hike to the southern boundary. Instead, the violator was marched, pushed, prodded and drug through 30 miles of rugged country even in the dead of winter and kicked out of the Park at the north entrance.

A common practice of Captain Harris' Troop was to deposit poachers in the local jail in Mammoth Hot Springs and then wire Washington for instructions. Communications were painfully (for the shackled) slow in those days, and it might take a week to get word back to fine and remove the poachers from the Park. And

One of the few places where a small herd of elk had survived the market hunters of the Plains was in the remote, rugged mountains of northwestern Wyoming where Yellowstone National Park now stands.

The few elk that had escaped the elk holocaust of the Plains were soon being slaughtered by poachers and market hunters who brazenly flaunted their illegal trade in front of outgunned Rangers in the early days of Yellowstone National Park. Photo National Park Service.

more than one elk butcher who thought he could stand up to the seasoned cavalry veterans was thoroughly thrashed.

Word got around quickly. Poaching itself became the endangered species, and illegal kills dropped to almost nothing. The hoped-for results were astounding. In just ten years, elk numbers approached 20,000 and continued to grow in spite of the occasional setback from an unusually bitter winter which took its toll on the elk.

However, those few small herds of elk hidden in remote pockets outside the Park still had little chance to increase because as soon as a few of these animals multiplied and ventured into the open, they were killed. This hopeless condition was witnessed and despised by a certain man who, at the time, could only stand by frustrated and helpless as the nation's treasure trove of natural resources was wasted.

The man's name was Theodore Roosevelt, and he was a firsthand witness to much of the near destruction of one of our nation's most valuable resources — its wildlife. As a private citizen he was limited, but as the President of the United States, Teddy Roosevelt wielded extraordinary power, and often a club, in his march to make right many of the environmental wrongs that had occurred in front of his own eyes.

Teddy Roosevelt was instrumental in the formation of a conservation program that became the nucleus of today's far-reaching system of protection of

Roosevelt's master plan was to use Yellowstone's rapidly growing elk herd as the seed crop to reintroduce elk back to many areas from where it had been eliminated. Photo courtesy of National Park Service.

our natural resources. He gathered a group of very influential men to help him. Their names comprise a veritable "Who's Who" of conservation patriarchs, including Aldo Leopold, Gifford Pinchot, General William Sherman and Congressman George Grinnell.

With the help of these far-seeing men, Roosevelt founded the Boone & Crockett Club, The National Park, National Forest and National Wildlife Refuge systems.

Roosevelt's master plan was to use Yellowstone National Park as a wildlife stock farm for elk. With the Park's protected elk herd healthy and growing fast, his strategy was to reintroduce his beloved elk back into areas from where it had been exterminated. But first, he had to make sure that any elk transplants were not slaughtered soon after they were reintroduced. In 1902, he was able to cajole Congress into placing a ten year moratorium on elk hunting anywhere in America.

By 1912, after a ten year federal moratorium on elk hunting in the West, the master plan of using the Yellowstone elk herd to reintroduce the species back into its former haunts had begun. Small bands of elk were rounded up and transported by rail and stock truck to points north, south, east and west. Even Canada was included. Between 1917 and 1920, a reintroduction plan for the Province of Alberta consisting of several hundred head of elk was accomplished, and that became the nucleus of Alberta's present elk herd, which numbers in the thousands.

The state of Colorado, once flush with elk herds, had also seen the species extirpated due to encroachment on habitat and unregulated market hunting. In 1912, that state began introducing elk into areas which once held large elk herds. This process continued through 1928 and the result has been hailed as one of the greatest elk management success stories of all time because today Colorado harbors a huge elk population of more than a quarter million animals.

Likewise, other western states such as Wyoming, Idaho, Montana, Oregon, Washington, Arizona, New Mexico and Nevada received Rocky Mountain elk from herds in Yellowstone National Park or the nearby National Elk Refuge in Jackson Hole, Wyoming.

By 1922, elk numbers were estimated at 90,000. The statewide moratorium on hunting was carefully lifted, and seasons were tightly controlled. The elk continued to flourish. By 1940 there were 200,000 elk, and by 1975 more than 500,000 elk roamed the land.

Still, there were nagging problems on the horizon. Many areas where elk formerly lived were barren of the species. And with the encroachment of civilization in the form of unregulated housing developments, ski areas and mines upon critical elk wintering range, more land was needed to be set aside so that future generations of elk could flourish. But more than that, education and

By the 1920's many western states had watched their seed crop of elk grow into the thousands. By 1922, elk numbers were estimated at 90,000 and increased to a half million by 1975.

sensitivity to the critical requirements of the elk were desperately needed. So once again, someone was needed to champion the cause of the elk.

Unfortunately, the great political conservationist and champion of the elk's cause, Teddy Roosevelt, had long ago passed from the earth. So had Aldo Leopold, Gifford Pinchot, William Sherman and George Grinnell. In these days of the "me" generation, was there anyone out there with fortitude, with resolve, with passion, and most of all, with courage?

Fortunately for the elk and for elk lovers throughout the world, a few such men still existed, but they carried no prestigious monikers such as "President" or "Congressman" or "Wealthy Philanthropist." If the elk was to survive and flourish into the new millennium, this time it would take common men who worked with their hands and toiled by the sweat of their brow. Yeh, just everyday guys, but when elk were mentioned, that "Roosevelt Glint" came to their eyes.

The ability of the elk to adapt to habitat variations throughout the vastness of the wild American West helped enable their recovery. Here a small band of elk are shown in a high mountain basin in the northern Rocky Mountains.

The Rocky Mountain Elk Foundation's headquarters and Visitor Center in Missoula, Montana is the focal point for one of the greatest conservation movements in America. Photo courtesy RMEF.

Chapter Six

The Rocky Mountain Elk Foundation Story

One of the greatest conservation success stories of modern times began in an ordinary place. Troy, Montana, is just a small town nestled among heavy forest, rolling mountains and ice cold streams.

Residents of Troy and the nearby town of Libby were just as ordinary. Logging and mining were the main industries, and these towns tended to reflect the humble, hard working personalities of these endeavors. But in 1984, something big was about to happen to the conservation world, and it would come out of the tiny town of Troy. And like so many of America's great success stories, its beginning was not only humble, but also precarious.

Four hunting buddies, brothers Bob and Bill Munson and friends Charlie Decker and Dan Bull were going about their lives as loggers, businessmen, realtors, when they began discussing the need for more care and thought to be given to the management of elk in their area and across the West.

Even though the elk had rebounded from its near extinction at the turn of the century, warning signs were popping up everywhere. After peaking in the mid-60s, some elk populations had begun to decline. As the West became popular as a clean place to live, and as more and more vacationers discovered it, much of the elk's critical winter habitat began to disappear under parking lots and condominiums.

In addition, subtle environmental changes were also occurring. Much of the brush that had sustained elk herds during the lean winter months had grown above the reach of the elk, leaving many animals to slowly starve under a sea of nourishing twigs and buds just out of reach. In addition, state and federal land use decisions and polices often overlooked the elk as a critical piece of the environmental puzzle.

The four friends felt both a frustration and void when it came to maintaining not only healthy elk herds, but also a national focus to bring elk lovers into the decision making process. After all, ducks had a dedicated bunch of folks looking out for waterfowl and their habitat. So did sheep, whitetails, quail, turkeys, trout and bass. These organizations had made a tremendous impact for the causes they represented. Literally millions of outdoorsmen belonged to this handful of conservation groups. But the elk had no one.

In March of 1984, these men took that first courageous step forward when they hired two consultants from Spokane, Washington, to help them put together their first direct-mail campaign. The consultants optimistically predicted a 5-10 percent return from this 43,000-piece mailing to elk hunters.

Bob, Charlie, Bill and Dan had no reason to doubt the consultants. Anticipating a flood of returns, Bob Munson even bid on a surplus automatic letter opener. He then cleared off a space in his Troy real estate office and plugged it in so it would be warmed up when the returns began to arrive at the office in those big white canvas mail bags. Actually, a small lunch bag would have held most of the returns. Reality began to rear its ugly head in the next week when less than one half of one percent signed on to this strange new organization called The Rocky Mountain Elk Foundation.

Still, the founders eagerly checked the mail each day, hoping for a late surge in memberships. Unfortunately, there were barely enough membership envelopes passing through the automatic letter opener to pay for the electricity it used. Desperate for support, Bob, Bill, and Charlie hopped a plane to Washington, D.C. "to learn how the big guys did it." Every day, Bob phoned his office hoping for good news. As gently as she could, his secretary Hilde Johnson told Bob that only one membership had arrived while he was gone. Hilde felt Bob's dejection and tried to sound optimistic. "We've had bad weather out here. The roads are icy, maybe the mail truck ran off the road." It was Rolaids time.

New RMEF members had been promised a first-class magazine dedicated to information about elk. However, none of the founders had any experience with magazine design, layout or cost. It's a good thing, too, because if they had, their hair probably would have turned white overnight!

When they discovered that the cost of producing the first issue of the RMEF's flagship publication, *Bugle* magazine, was $25,000, the guys almost fainted! Undaunted, Bob Munson asked his good friend, pilot Bob Marmaduke, for a $25,000 loan. On a wing and a prayer, Marmaduke agreed. But that was just the beginning of the bad news. After they rushed the check to the printer, they were informed that the cost had nearly doubled to $48,000. More Rolaids!

In the meantime, the founders had hired Lance Schelvan, then a graphic specialist working for the U.S. Forest Service in Libby, to put together the first issue of *Bugle* magazine. Lance quickly began calling every wildlife biologist and outdoor writer he knew to contribute an article to the magazine, and he contacted every elk-related industry to buy advertising space.

Following a lead, Lance and Bob literally discovered the pot at the end of the rainbow in Minnesota's Hart Press. Despite grave misgivings about this zealous bunch from Montana who already emptied their own savings accounts and were borrowed to the hilt, Hart Press's Bob Blasing took on the new account.

Lance quickly threw together that first issue and finally "pasted up" all the editorial and advertising. But Lance's method used scotch-taping the photos and columns in place. The printer quickly called back and gently informed the guys that the scotch tape had created an incredible glare in the printing process, burning out letters, even entire words. But time had run out. The premiere inaugural issue of *Bugle* magazine would have to go to press "as-is."

In a few weeks, a truck arrived in Troy, burdened with 35,000 issues of *Bugle* magazine. The Munson brothers, Charlie Decker and John Marmaduke stood silently as Marmaduke opened the premiere issue. John carefully perused through the pages for a few minutes, studying what his $25,000 investment had wrought. Finally he spoke. "It'll never sell."

No man likes to be a false prophet, but in this case, John Marmaduke was only too happy to take back his initial gloomy assessment. *Bugle* magazine did sell. Despite the slight blemishes in design, that first issue contained real editorial meat. It began exploring the dilemma of elk in Yellowstone National Park. Conservationists, animal lovers and elk enthusiasts finally had a publication that did more than show pretty pictures of wildlife. Through the years, *Bugle* has risen to the top as a literary conservation magazine. Besides breathtaking photography, each issue is chock-full of sensitive articles about the interrelationships between man and elk, in-depth issues on elk biology and conservation news.

Still, back in 1985 when the RMEF was in its infancy, the founders felt a necessity to bring all factions on the issues of elk and their habitat to one grand

During this ceremony, the Robb Creek property in southwestern Montana is dedicated, thanks to a corporate sponsorship contribution from Anheuser-Busch, Inc. L-R, Wallace Pate, First Chairman of the Board of the RMEF; Jim Flynn, Director of Montana Fish, Wildlife, Parks; Ray Goff, Vice President, Anheuser-Busch; Bob Munson, RMEF President. The Rocky Mountain Elk Foundation has purchased, or helped set aside, many land parcels that were critical elk habitat, and then turned these lands over to state officials. A total of 2.3 million acres have been conserved for elk and other wildlife. Photo courtesy RMEF.

meeting. They called for the inaugural Rocky Mountain Elk Foundation Convention in nearby Spokane, Washington. Great idea, scary logistics. No sooner had they set up the convention, when the enormous chore of such a venture struck the men. Hundreds of people would be needed to pull off this convention, so the small RMEF staff quickly rounded up friends, families, volunteers — anyone who had a passion for elk and elk hunting. "We weren't selective back in those days," recalled Bob Munson. "If you had a pulse, you could have a job."

However, the vastness of the undertaking in Spokane often got the best of Bob Munson and Charlie Decker. More than once, Munson remembers the two men sitting in their cars watching visitors trickle into the convention center — with the motor running and the quickest route back to Troy plotted on the road map in front of them.

But a fast getaway wasn't needed. They filled all the advertising booth spaces, and not one of the 3,000 registered guests filed a complaint. And why should they? The RMEF had managed to assemble some of the most impressive elk racks in the world, trucking them in from Alberta, Colorado, Montana and Wyoming.

They'd also convinced well-known biologists Jack Ward Thomas and Gary Wolfe to speak on the nature and status of elk in America. Noted elk bowhunter Larry D. Jones gave an elk hunting seminar, and humorist Patrick McManus, who lives in Spokane, also agreed to come.

The first RMEF advisory committee gathered at the convention, made up of, as Bob says, "anyone with a big name in elk hunting circles." Originally, those names included Canadian outfitter Lyle Dorey, Montana writer and book publisher Dale Burk, Arizona hunting expert Mike Cupell, nationally known hunter Jim Zumbo and biologist Gary Wolfe.

That unexpected show of support at the first convention kept Bob and Charlie from shifting into drive until the convention was over. Obviously, the founders had struck a chord in the hearts of a huge, hibernating hoard of elk lovers. Membership applications began to dribble in. Then it became a steady trickle. Then it became a steady stream. Eventually, it would became a movement as large as any conservation effort in the history of North America.

Today, the annual Rocky Mountain Elk Foundation convention is a gala affair often attended by more than 30,000 elk lovers. Hundreds of exhibitors offer a variety of wares ranging from hunting equipment to fine wildlife art and jewelry. Some of the most prominent authorities in the world on wildlife and elk offer insights through a succession of seminars during the day, and everything from old-fashioned barn dances to big name entertainment is offered in the evening.

As previously mentioned, the founders were working men who chafed at the way other organizations often took members' money, but then returned very little of the promised conservation money back to the land. They were determined to become a conservation group whose main emphasis, workwise and moneywise, was to help the elk and its habitat.

That's what attracted Alberta outfitter Lyle Dorey to the RMEF during its infancy. "I drove down to Troy to check this new outfit out myself," Lyle recalls. "I was very impressed with the commitment to the elk and to the membership that these founders had in those early days. They had a passion to do everything right and avoid the mistakes of other groups."

From the start, the RMEF has been hands-on and elk-dedicated — even when there was virtually no money in the treasury. Bob Munson recalls that in the beginning, their first elk project expenditure was money for a tank of gas to have elk transplanted from Yellowstone National Park to Montana.

Through the years, the Rocky Mountain Elk Foundation has grown, and grown, and grown. It now totals more than 115,000 members worldwide and has generated more than $70 million to enhance elk habitat, acquire critical elk habitat, and fund important wildlife research and conservation education programs.

But its principal objectives remain the same — to help conserve elk and their habitat. Case in point: while some other groups are so top-heavy that most of their revenue is used to support their internal bureaucracies, the RMEF spends an average of more than 90 cents of every dollar toward furthering the RMEF's mission of ensuring the future of elk, other wildlife and their habitat. How many other organizations can claim such a lofty commitment?

Though its work has primarily been concentrated in the western states because that's where most of the elk are found, the RMEF has not forgotten that elk once roamed over most of North America. Many habitat improvements and elk

The governor of Wisconsin releases the first RMEF sponsored elk transplant to that state. The Rocky Mountain Elk Foundation has helped reintroduce the elk back to many of its former haunts. Photo courtesy RMEF.

transplants have been completed with RMEF funds or cooperation in rather surprising places, such as Arkansas, Pennsylvania, Kansas, Minnesota, Wisconsin, Kentucky and Ontario, Canada.

Any lands acquired by the RMEF to protect critical elk habitat are usually transferred or sold to public management agencies, thereby safeguarding public access and the land's wildlife values. To date, the RMEF has helped acquire critical habitat in sixteen states and three Canadian provinces. In large part due to these heroics, plus an aggressive campaign to educate the public about the need for critical habitat, the North American elk herd has nearly doubled since 1975.

The RMEF has recognized that the future of the elk depends upon conservation education, and they have taken a giant step toward attaining the goal of teaching the next generation about wildlife conservation and stewardship. In 1996, the RMEF purchased and renamed a kids conservation magazine, calling it *WOW™ (Wild Outdoor World)*. This beautiful magazine is full of colorful, entertaining and educational stories about wildlife and habitat conservation. Wild Outdoor World Magazine™ targets 8 to 12-year-olds, and is currently being distributed to fourth-grade classrooms in several states, free of charge, to be used as a teaching tool. It has already won a Silver and a Gold Award from the Parents' Choice Foundation, considered to be the "Oscars" of children's media and toys,

Thanks in large part to the Rocky Mountain Elk Foundation's conservation work, today's elk population hovers at a million.

as well as four Distinguished Achievement Awards for excellence in educational journalism from the Educational Press of America.

But neither has the Rocky Mountain Elk Foundation's dynamic energy and conservation success gone unnoticed, resulting in several prestigious awards, including the 1991 Chevron Conservation Award, the United Nations Environment Programs Award for 1996, the U.S. Department of Interior-B.L.M. Health of the Land Award of 1996, the Renewable Natural Resources Foundation's Outstanding Achievement Award, and others. In addition, large corporations have also lent support. Anheuser-Busch Company was one of the first large corporate supporters, with a $500,000 donation to acquire critical elk habitat on the Robb Creek property in southwestern Montana. Since then, many corporations have joined with the RMEF's conservation effort.

However, the RMEF's management is quick to identify the source of its success — its vast volunteer corps. More than 10,000 folks volunteer their time and effort in a variety of conservation and fund-raising ventures annually. In Nevada, it may be a local RMEF chapter building water guzzlers for elk and other wildlife in the parched Nevada desert. In South Dakota, it may be a local chapter erecting an elk-proof fence to keep elk out of a farmer's crop field.

In addition, a volunteer-led annual banquet program among the RMEF's

The programs that helped preserve and develop quality habitat for elk in turn helped develop healthy herds.

nearly 500 chapters in forty-nine states and five Canadian provinces raises about $10 million each year for elk and other wildlife habitat. These hard-working people are the pulse and identity of the RMEF. When the rest of North America sees the hard work and generosity of these volunteers, they want to become a part of such a selfless movement. Is it, then, any wonder why the RMEF has come to epitomize the ideal non-profit conservation organization?

There you have it. Four buddies in a small town had a dream. In just fourteen years, that dream has spawned 115,000 members, conserved 2.3 million acres, completed more than 2,000 conservation projects, funded a variety of wildlife research and education, and helped return elk herds to some states where they haven't existed for 130-150 years. But most importantly, the RMEF has shown the way for an increasingly indifferent American public to return to the methods and dedication of those early conservationists at the turn of the century.

I'm not a great one for joining fraternal organizations rife with molding rhetoric and stodgy, cigar-smoking elitists. But I am a member of the Rocky Mountain Elk Foundation. Why not become a part of this great conservation effort? For more information, call the Rocky Mountain Elk Foundation at 1-800-Call ELK or write:

The Rocky Mountain Elk Foundation
P.O. Box 8249
Missoula, Montana 59807-8249

RMEF Mission Statement

The mission of the Rocky Mountain Elk Foundation is to ensure the future of elk, other wildlife and their habitat.

In support of this mission, the RMEF is committed to:

1. Conserving, restoring, and embracing natural habitats.

2. Promoting the sound management of wild, free-ranging elk and other wildlife, which may be hunted or otherwise enjoyed.

3. Fostering cooperation among federal, state and private organizations and individuals in wildlife management and habitat conservation.

4. Educating members and the public about habitat conservation, the value of hunting, hunting ethics, and wildlife management.

Chapter Seven

Elk Predators

All elk die a violent death. Whether it is by claw or fang, or the impact of a bullet, an elk's life is destined from birth to end traumatically. In the natural world, there is no such thing as dying peacefully. The law of the jungle, or in this case the forest, decries that only the fittest survive. This axiom also holds true for the elk. The swift, the strong, and the more wary of the species are able to avoid the fierce rush of the grizzly, or break away from the dagger-like claws of the lion, or slip away unnoticed from the hunter. But sooner or later, the elk will make a mistake, and then the law of the jungle presides.

In time, even the strongest and quickest elk is eventually slowed by the harsh environment that he lives in, and he falls prey to the host of predators who lie in wait. But even if the predator is removed, hunting is stopped — and the elk is allowed to live to old age, death is still by no means pleasant. Elk do not die a natural death, by human standards. After years of grinding grass and browse, an older elk's teeth will have been worn below the gums, making it increasingly difficult to feed. The ultimate fate of an aged elk in the wild is to slowly starve to death.

I've watched elk in early spring in Yellowstone National Park endure the slow eating away of their bodies because they could not take in enough food to maintain sufficient nourishment. As their own body begins to be consumed, their eyes become sunken, their ribs begin to show, and their gait becomes unsteady as the muscle and marrow in their bones is consumed.

I've watched this spectacle many times, and it never ceases to affect me. I am forced to remind myself that this is how the cycle of nature works. The strong survive, and the weak die. Still, it is an unnerving thing for this well-fed human to watch an elk slowly starve to death over a two week period. Anyone who believes that if elk would just be left alone, then the species could live a peaceful existence, should schedule a trip to Yellowstone about April 1st when the Park Service is using a front end loader to scoop carcasses from the roads and load them into trucks to be dumped somewhere far away from the noses of urban tourists ignorant to how nature truly works in our national parks.

Unfortunately, there are individuals who fail to see how nature's perfect cycle operates with precise severity to maintain a proper carrying population in the land. I once watched a group of early season tourists, who had come upon a starving bull elk along the road to Lamar Valley in Yellowstone, rummage through

their packs and place a bagful of chips on the ground in front of the glassy-eyed elk's snout. A few hours later, the great bull elk finally died. And no, he hadn't sampled any of the potato chips.

It is critically important that any nature lover fully understand the true cycle of nature if he or she wants to appreciate how wonderful and perfect this earth and its wildlife function as one huge ecosystem. In the natural world, innocent blood is often spilled by another innocent creature to sustain that species, while controlling over-population of another species. And yes, even that most curious of all animal species, man, is a player in this perpetual drama.

Elk predation can be attributed to four major species — the mountain lion (cougar), bears (grizzly and black), the wolf, and man. Each species exacts a certain toll on the elk, and each has its own hunting technique that is unique to the species and depends on the strengths of that particular species. To the intelligent human, reared in a democratic society where aggressive behavior is punished, many of these animals' actions may appear to be unbearably cruel and murderous. But if these acts of predation are taken as necessary acts to perpetuate a healthy elk herd overall, a spectator to the sight of a baby elk being joyfully torn apart by a predator can eventually look on this seemingly savage act as a necessary piece of the puzzle of nature.

Mountain Lion

The mountain lion is found throughout elk country in the West, where there are an estimated 15,000 lions roaming the land. Its population in most states is steadily growing, and it is slowly reclaiming much of the western landscape from which it had disappeared.

The largest mature male lions, called toms, will weigh only about 190 pounds, and most average about thirty pounds less. A female lion will tip the scales at about 90-120 pounds. But don't be fooled by these smallish weights, for its size belies this animal's ability as a predator.

A lion is the epitome of the hunter as it slips silently through the forest, always on the alert, always watching. Its body is perfectly built for the hunt. Its legs are short, which allows it to keep its body low to the ground where prey cannot easily spot it. Often times, a fallen tree or a rotting log eighteen inches in diameter is enough to conceal the deadly stalk of the lion.

Though its legs are short, its body is rather long, often eight feet from its nose to the tip of its tail. This allows it to cover great distances with blinding speed. Observers who have witnessed a lion's charge describe it as nothing less than a tawny blur.

Much of the lion's hunting prowess can be attributed to its muscular structure. A skinned mountain lion's carcass reveals a body taut with bulging muscles. Tremendous foreleg muscles which end at dagger-like claws attest to the lion's formidable ability to inflict swift, deadly damage. One of the most impressive muscles is found in the lion's jaws. Huge canine teeth are powered by a fist-sized ball of muscle tucked behind each lower jawbone.

nawed rib bones stand in stark testimony that all elk die a violent death, whether it is claw or fang, or the impact of a bullet, or a brutal winter — an elk's life is destined end traumatically.

Currently, the mountain lion is probably responsible for more elk predation mortality than any other predator.

I live in lion country, and I often travel unarmed through its hunting territory. I always felt that, as a former football player and over-all tough guy, I certainly could beat off the attack of a puny ninety pound lion. But after I'd inspected the skinned carcass of a lion who had been destroyed for killing a 1,500 pound cow, I gulped and had to admit that there was probably much more packaged in that hundred pound frame than I could handle.

When it is in its hunting mode, a lion silently glides through the forest, often seeking ridge points or the edge of an opening, where its keen eyesight can spot the slightest movement hundreds of yards away. When it spots an elk, the lion quickly appraises the cover and wind direction, and then circles to get the wind in its face and begins its stalk through cover that affords the best concealment.

A stalking lion is a sight to behold. It flits between openings so quickly that the untrained eye may not even be able to identify it as a lion. As the lion closes on its quarry, it begins moving slowly forward, stopping often behind the slightest bit of cover. A log, a stump, even a small bush, is enough for the lion to conceal its ground hugging stalk. When the lion is within sixty yards of its quarry, it begins a slow, belly-crawling advance that has it moving forward in spurts. When the feeding animal has its head down, the lion may move forward a few paces, but then freezes when the animal picks up its head.

At thirty yards, it is within striking distance. It bunches its legs and appears as a huge coil, trembling with anticipation. When the animal lowers its head to feed, the lion leaps forward in a blur of movement. Often times, the startled prey is able to stumble only a few bounds before the lion is there.

The lion tries to lunge onto the elk's neck, where its long claws dig in, and it adheres to the fleeing elk like glue. The lion then bites into the back of the neck, thereby stabilizing the neck from further movement. The lion then reaches around

ften times, a fallen log is enough to conceal the deadly stalk of a lion.

and hooks the elk's snout with its dew (thumb) claw, a large curved claw growing out of the lion's paw near the middle of its wrist. The lion then wrenches the elk's head down and back in one powerful jerk and breaks its neck.

A lion's attack does not resemble a wild rodeo ride through the woods. If everything goes right, the lion's attack, and elk's broken neck, occur within seconds. But not every lion hunt ends successfully. Maybe one elk in five is killed, and I have observed four different elk with long scars along their shoulders and flanks, where a lion's charge fell short of making it to the critical neck area before the elk bolted.

Still, the notion of a ninety pound female lion successfully hunting an 800 pound bull elk seems absurd. In fact, it is, if the two faced off and met in the arena. But that's not the lion's way. It relies on stealth, surprise and technique. And yes, a ninety pound lion can and will kill the largest bull elk because it utilizes its strengths against the mighty elk's weakness which, of course, is its neck.

A friend of mine, Larry Bennett, told me that one day while elk hunting in the snow covered mountains of western Montana, he spotted a disturbance in the snow on a steep, tree-covered hillside. As he approached the spot, Larry noticed fresh lion tracks also headed in that direction. He could see where the lion's tracks suddenly spaced out into a gallop, until it got to the site of the disturbance, where it coincided with a set of huge elk tracks.

Larry searched the open forest below for a hundred yards, but saw nothing except a long trough tunnelled through snow, complete with kicked-up dirt and small trees uprooted. Larry had followed the trough for about 150 yards, when he stepped over a large blowdown and discovered the freshly killed carcass of a mature six point bull elk covered with snow and twigs. The lion had fed on the left rear hindquarter, and then had covered the carcass to hide it from scavengers and birds.

Larry told me from the zig-zag appearance of the trough, there had been a titanic, bloody struggle between lion and bull elk. Larry guessed that the bull's large rack of antlers probably kept the lion from making a quick neck break, and the huge disturbance at the kill site attested to an intense, final struggle for the hapless bull elk.

Being a supreme predator, the lion is always on the lookout for an easy kill. For the most part, life is not easy for the lion. Days may go by between kills, and sometimes stretches into a week or more, whereupon a lion is reduced to eating berries or vegetation to fuel its body for the next hunt. It exists on the razor's edge between a gluttonous banquet of elk or deer meat, and the gnawing pain of a shrunken, empty stomach.

Usually, a lion consumes most, or all, of a fallen prey before it ventures off to hunt again. However, at certain times of the year, such as the deep snows of late winter, a lion can wreak havoc with a wintering animal herd and kill much more than it needs to survive. This usually occurs when game herds are forced by deep snow to move down to bottom lands where snow depth is less. This

Bears are opportunists. They eat grass to survive, but prefer meat. They'll feed on putrid animal carcass, but they're also not above "creating" a carcass with a sudd? rush at an unsuspecting elk.

concentrates the preoccupied, hungry animals. It also offers too much of a temptation for the opportunistic mountain lion to pass up.

Lion hunter Larry Bennett told me about a wildlife biologist who was studying a particular female lion with two yearling cubs, who discovered a small draw where a large herd of elk were eking out a meager existence in late February, deep-snow conditions. The researcher found where the female lion had stalked and killed four cow elk in one morning, eating only a small portion of each elk before moving on. The researcher believed that this particular female lion was showing her sub-adult offspring how to hunt.

Presently, the mountain lion is responsible for more elk predation than any other four-legged hunter in America. That's because the lion is constantly hunting, unlike the bear, whose diet also consists of many other things besides meat. (Wolf populations in western states have not grown large enough, yet, but with increasing wolf packs, expect the wolf to soon overtake the lion in elk kills.) Biologists estimate that a mature lion will make a kill about every ten days. If it is an elk kill in the winter, when the meat will stay fresh, the lion may feed on the elk for a few weeks before seeking other prey, but if it is in summer, the lion may only feed for a few days because lions do not like to eat putrefied meat.

Bears

Bears are omnivorous, meaning they eat both vegetation and meat. Actually, bears eat plants and grass to survive, but they prefer meat, and lots of it — fresh or putrid. They're only too happy to dive into the middle of a week-old elk carcass, but being an opportunist, a bear is always on the lookout for an easy meal and is not above "creating" a carcass with a sudden charge at an unwary animal.

Most elk predation from bears comes in late spring when the cow elk are calving. The cows move to certain birthing areas tucked back away from civilization where their babies will have the best chance for survival. This usually occurs about the first week in June. This is a period of rejoicing of the renewal of the species, but it is also a killing field for the bears.

Both black bears and grizzlies hunt newborn elk calves, but the black bear is especially cautious in grizzly country because the grizzly can, and will, make a meal of any black bear it comes across. In areas where the grizzly is not found, black bears are especially hard on the newborn elk crop. One study done in a birthing area of central Idaho discovered that upwards to 40 percent of newborn elk calves were being killed by black bears.

However, it is the grizzly who is most prominent in our national parks as it roams the elk birthing areas, much like a bird dog, sniffing out the scent of newborns. Unlike the buffalo calf, which can keep up with the adults after a week, an elk calf needs about three weeks before it can outrun a bear. But even then, it's a close race for survival.

You'd think that an elk, even a young one, could easily outrun the rolly-polly grizzly bear. But it comes as a shock to an observer the first time they see a pot-bellied grizzly running at full speed. Even over rough terrain, a grizzly can maintain a speed of about thirty-five miles per hour over a long distance.

I watched an amazing display of a grizzly in action a few years ago. I was videoing grizzlies in Yellowstone National Park for an upcoming video titled "Bear

Attacks. " I'd settled down for a peaceful evening of glassing the open slopes, when a 300 pound grizzly suddenly emerged from the timber and began roaming back and forth over an area where several cow elk had hidden their babies.

The elk immediately stampeded, and the grizzly gave chase, but the elk had at least a 300 yard head start, so I knew it was a hopeless chase for the bear. But the bear never gave up. After a while, it was 200 yards back, then 100 yards. All of a sudden, the bear found an extra gear and put on a burst of speed. The cow easily outran the bear, but the poor calf was finally thundered to the ground with a hammer-like swat from the bear. The frantic cow screamed and pleaded from no more than fifteen yards away, but the grizzly ignored her as he contentedly tore the calf elk apart.

The next day when I returned to the area, that grizzly was on a different calf elk kill. Two days later, I spotted the grizzly feeding on yet another carcass a half mile away. I've lived much of my life among the wild animals, and I'm cognizant of the austere techniques of Mother Nature. Still, it is enough to choke you up inside when you see the wholesale slaughter of a beautiful baby elk, and you hear the anguished pleading of a mother that has just lost her calf.

An adult elk can easily outrun a grizzly bear, so elk predation by grizzly bears falls off after the calving season, but the opportunistic grizzly still occasionally catches a careless elk. One spring, I watched as a herd of elk feeding

Bears that roam the elk's calving grounds take a fearful number of newborn calves in the three weeks before the calves are strong enough to outrun a bear.

along the swollen Lamar River was suddenly charged by a grizzly that had stalked to within 200 yards before galloping out of a gully. The elk herd stampeded downstream diagonally away from the bear. That was enough of an edge for the fast-closing grizzly. He knocked a large cow senseless with one crushing blow, and the stunned animal catapulted into the river. The grizzly jumped in and dragged the cow out of the river and up thirty feet of steep bank before it proceeded to tear it apart.

An Indian guide from Canada also told me that grizzlies often hunted elk in his area by lying in ambush along well-used game trails and then charging passing elk. He added that grizzlies often were attracted to elk by a rutting bull's bugle, or a hunter's call. In fact, some grizzlies have even come to associate an elk hunter's gunshot as a call to dinner because they'd begun to associate the bang of a rifle with a dead elk. A few years ago, two rifle hunters in British Columbia who'd just killed a bull elk were attacked, killed and partially eaten by a grizzly that had sneaked in while the men were field dressing the elk.

And forget the notion that a mature bull elk can stand up to the fierce charge of a grizzly bear. Such a battle would last just seconds and end immediately when the grizzly landed one of its mighty, sledge-hammer blows. In a test of strength and power, there is no equal to the grizzly in America, and the elk's best defense against the great bear is flight — and sometimes that's not even enough.

Wolves

The wolf is a good predator match for an elk. Unlike the bear and lion, which lack the speed and stamina of a galloping elk over long distance, wolves hunting in a pack are able to literally run down a mature elk. Still, it's very difficult for a single wolf to take down an elk, so wolves hunt in packs totalling anywhere from two to eight animals. Whether it is through practice, or instinct, the wolf pack utilizes a cunningly effective hunting technique of encirclement, interception and speed to hunt their prey.

Last spring in Yellowstone Park, I had the privilege of observing this hunting technique as the Slough Creek wolf pack, consisting of three gray and two black wolves, hunted a herd of elk near the Lamar River.

The wolves had trotted out onto a low ridge and paced back and forth while the large light-gray alpha male stood stoically by himself, studying several elk feeding about 500 yards away. Finally, the alpha male and another gray wolf, probably the alpha female, began trotting diagonally toward the elk. When I looked back, the other wolves had disappeared.

The two wolves advanced to within three hundred yards before the nervous elk began trotting away. The two wolves began running after the elk in half-hearted fashion. The elk had easily outdistanced the two wolves and were about to top a ridge and disappear from sight, when the herd suddenly scattered. It was then that I saw the other three wolves charge into view over the ridgetop.

A large cow veered off diagonally back downhill by herself, quartering away from the two gray wolves. Suddenly, all five wolves put it into overdrive, and I was amazed at their speed. One of the black wolves was able to overtake the

...ven though the wolf's speed and agility are a good match for a fleeing elk, a lone wolf ...ually can't take down an elk. That's why wolves usually hunt in packs.

cow and it must have bit at her flank because she kicked and spun to her right. In the meantime, the gray alpha male had put on a tremendous burst of speed and overtook the cow. With a breathtaking leap, the wolf landed on the cow's shoulder and sank his fangs into her neck. Both animals somersaulted through the sagebrush, but before the cow could regain her feet, the other wolves were on her, tearing and ripping. In less than a minute the cow's attempts to rise had ceased and she lay gasping her last breaths. A few of the wolves were already gulping down huge chunks of meat torn from her hams. For me, it had been breathtaking, thrilling — and horrible — all at once.

The next day, I witnessed one of the most perplexing examples of elk behavior, and it left me wondering if, indeed, I understood these animals at all. I sat 300 yards away from this elk kill with my camera equipped with 400mm telephoto lens, waiting for the wolves to return. Two cow elk fed over toward me, but when they spotted me, they became instantly alert and trotted off about 400 yards, barking a warning for at least an hour. They continued to be very wary and suspicious of me.

My attention was torn away from the two elk when the wolves returned to the carcass, which was on the far side of the Lamar River. As the wolf pack playfully pulled at what was left from yesterday's feeding, those two cow elk sauntered up to the edge of the Lamar River and watched the wolves feed — not

In a "death wish" move, these two elk curiously advance to within a hundred yards of a pack of wolves feeding on a recent elk kill — and become the wolves' next meal.

more than seventy yards away! That was too much of a temptation for the big alpha male. After eyeing the elk for a few minutes he began to swim the river toward them. He was halfway across before the elk decided to run! They easily outdistanced the trailing alpha male, but when I looked back, the other wolves were nowhere in sight.

I don't know what instinct would make those two elk so alert to my presence, yet would draw them literally into the jaws of the wolf pack. To me, it's just further proof that we haven't learned all there is to know about the elk.

Besides the Yellowstone wolves, several new wolf packs have also been reintroduced into Idaho and Montana. In addition, Mexican gray wolves have recently been released in Arizona, and they have already begun preying on elk.

While the newly arrived Yellowstone wolves have been getting most of the attention in recent years, it is a fact that natural wolf reintroduction into the West's ecosystems had begun at least two decades before. At the time when the first wolves arrived in holding pens at the Park, there were already a couple dozen wolf packs in western Montana and North Idaho hunting deer and elk.

Actually, I had my first wolf experience way back in 1972. One fall morning, I was listening to two bull elk bugle from a brushy sidehill in the remote North Fork Clearwater River drainage of North Idaho, when two wolves suddenly began howling a few hundred yards away. The two bulls immediately left the area, and I went back to excitedly inform officials of my discovery. My news was received with a smirk and the quip, "There are no wolves in Idaho."

Yet I began hearing stories of wolf sightings and predation, and I started investigating these occurrences. Better than half of them were authentic, in my opinion. When I moved to Montana, I began investigating wolf sightings in that state through the 1980's. More than once, I sat across a rickety old kitchen table sipping coffee with an old farmer until he trusted me enough to relate how he'd found a wolf or two attacking his cows or horses, and how the farmer had turned those killer wolves into "good wolves."

In 1986, in the state of Idaho, where supposedly no wolves existed, I photographed a yearling elk killed by two wolves, photographed a track in the snow with a dollar bill next to it as comparison, and mailed the photos to the wildlife biologist at the Avery Ranger District in the St. Joe National Forest. He later phoned me and stated, "Yes, that was a wolf kill, and they'd better get serious about dealing with this endangered species."

Obviously, a small but growing population of wolves have been preying on elk for the last three decades and were rapidly approaching Yellowstone country naturally. Be that as it may, it is still thrilling to see the fast-growing wolf population in the Park.

Interestingly, the wolves in Yellowstone prey on elk almost exclusively because they are the most numerous prey species, while the wolves in western Montana prey mostly on deer. A study done on the wolf packs in the North Fork Flathead River near Glacier National Park found that ninety percent of their prey was the whitetail deer because that species was most abundant and easier to hunt. Elk, moose and a variety of other animals made up the other ten percent of the wolves' diet.

Humans

Human predation occurs in two forms — hunting and habitat encroachment. Hunting has the greatest immediate impact on the elk herd, while uncontrolled development of critical winter elk habitat is responsible for a much greater impact on the elk herd in the long term.

Every western state has some type of hunting season for elk, depending upon the condition and size of the elk herd. For instance, in Colorado where the flourishing elk herd numbers over a quarter of a million, the hunting harvest is about 50,000 animals annually. In Nevada, where a relatively small elk herd exists, the harvest is only 200 elk.

Every hunting area is carefully managed by wildlife biologists with an eye for regulation and management of the elk as a renewable resource. In the major elk states, hunting revenues approach the tens of millions of dollars and contribute greatly to the economy of these states, with some of the revenue going to the continued research and expansion of elk habitat.

On the other hand, the question of whether elk should be hunted becomes a moot point if housing developments and condominiums take over the habitat where the elk need to live during those brutal winter months when survival is often tentative.

In fact, state and federal officials are now taking a much closer look at new developments that might adversely impact winter elk range, such as subdivisions, resorts or ski areas. Architectural plans are often modified to accommodate both human activity and the needs of the elk.

Conclusion

A host of predators impact the elk herd. Most of this predation is minimal, but combined, it keeps the overall elk herd trimmed to its habitat-carrying capacity. Even the large hunter harvest of elk has not adversely impacted the elk because every hunting state has shown a marked increase in their elk numbers over the past ten years. This is due mainly to hunting dollars, and the Rocky Mountain Elk Foundation, working to acquire and improve habitat. The one problem area for the existence of the elk remains habitat encroachment. If the secretive elk does not have enough land to live on when the winter snows force the herds to move down to the lower country where snow is less deep, the elk herds in those areas slowly diminish and eventually disappear.

ell regulated sport hunting helps keep the elk from overpopulating their immediate
abitat. The more serious human threat comes from the encroachment of civilization on
itical elk habitat.

Chapter Eight

The Secret Life Of The Elk Herd

Elk are very social animals. Unlike deer, which tend to only loosely associate with each other, elk live within a strong family group, called a herd, which may number anywhere from a half dozen animals to a hundred. Within that herd are several generations of offspring, and among those offspring is a well-structured pecking order.

Except for those few weeks during the rut, bull and cow elk live a segregated life. The mature bulls prefer to live in bachelor groups far back from the main herd, often tucked away in such remote high country that it is almost impossible to locate them. At times, a bachelor group will choose the highest tundra above timberline where summer storms and gale force winds buffet them almost daily, but where they find isolation and stress-free living conditions.

Within the bachelor herd, the larger bulls exert their dominance over the lesser bulls by using aggressive gestures, along with pushing and striking subordinates with their hooves. During the period when their antlers are in velvet and very sensitive, the bulls are careful to avoid antler contact. Actually, most of this pecking order among the bulls is more of a psychological thing carried over from dominance battles of the previous fall.

This harassment gets so severe for some of the younger bulls, that they leave the bachelor herd and stay by themselves, or they might join the main herd of cows lower down the mountain. On occasion, several of these immature bulls will band together and create their own teenage (so to speak) bachelor group. It is interesting to observe these younger bulls in this group. The same intense harassment that forced these younger bulls to leave in the first place, they, in turn, now mete out to lesser bulls within this immature bachelor group. For that reason, the smaller-bodied spikes, plus an occasional four point bull, may decide to leave the males behind and join the main elk herd consisting of cows and calves.

Unfortunately, they often must pay a price for this lowest level of the pecking order. A spike bull among a herd of cows is not looked upon by the females as a dominant animal. In fact, the mature cows tend to treat the spike bull as a subordinate, replete with occasional harassment and other dominance acts, such as forcing the young bull to stay on the outskirts of the herd, or constantly chasing him away from the better feeding areas.

*he secret life of the elk herd is discovered only by the quiet observer who spends much
ne in elk country during the four seasons of the year.*

Elk tend to be individuals, much like humans, and an immature bull that cannot withstand the harassment of older bulls within a bachelor group, and eventually ends up as a subordinate in a herd of cows, tends to be affected psychologically by this early submissive behavior. That's why a mature herd bull that has domination over all the cows and other bulls in a drainage during the rut may not be the most impressive physical specimen. Instead, he probably endured the harassment of the older bulls during his immature period. And having learned how to dominate an adversary from this intense early training, he began to exert domination with learned gestures and acts against other bulls his own size. Such a bull is destined to become a dominant personality within the elk herd.

Bull elk emit a variety of sounds. Of course, the most recognizable call of the bull elk is the bugle. This is a loud musical call with a hollow tone which the bulls make when the elk rut begins. This call not only serves to warn other bulls to stay away, but it also serves to make any receptive cows in the area aware of the bull's presence. Though the elk bugle is most common during the elk rut, I've heard bull elk emit a soft version of a bugle in summer and spring when they are startled or when upset, though this non-rut bugle lacks the fire and emotion of the rutting bugle.

Another common sound made by a rutting herd bull is called "glucking."

Except for a few weeks during the mating season when they seek cows, bull elk prefer to live in bachelor groups. These three large Colorado bulls are the patriarchs of a summer bachelor group of nine bulls.

As the herd bull attends to his harem of cows, he makes a low squishy, throaty noise that sounds like "gluck, gluck, gluck." This is a strange, surreal sound that only an observer close to a herd bull attending his cows in heat will hear.

I've also heard younger bulls emit a loud squeal when play-fighting with competitors. After the velvet is shed from their antlers, these younger bulls often engage in playful jousting matches while squealing softly, as if to unnerve their competitor.

A dominant bull also emits a loud hissing sound when he is very angry. This hissing tends to sound slurred and resembles "SH-SH-SH-SH." The bull makes this sound through his teeth as he advances toward an opponent with his head up and eyes rolling. This sound of impending battle is not only made by rutting bulls, but also by bulls in summer bachelor groups exerting their domination over lesser bulls.

An alerted bull makes two sounds. One is called a "Euch" — a clipped, loud, throaty squeal. A bull usually euches when he is suspicious of danger. When the bull identifies the danger, he then barks a louder, more guttural, euch resembling the bark of a dog.

The main elk herd, the one that is most visible in the lower country, consists of cows and calves. Generally, the elk within a specific herd stay with that unit for most of their lives and the majority of the animals will be biologically

Adult cows treat a newcomer harshly when it first joins the new herd. However, even the meanest old cow will accept and nuzzle a new calf.

related, though elk exhibit no family type of affection for each other, except for that brief period of intense affection and protection that a cow shows toward her calf. However, this bonding begins to rapidly wane soon after the calf is weaned, though a young elk may stay closely associated with its mother until next year's mating season begins.

Occasionally, a cow may become separated from her biological herd and will readily join a different group of elk. When this happens, the stranger is met with suspicion and must stay on the outskirts of the new herd until her smell and presence becomes familiar to the other members of that herd. During this time, she will be treated rather harshly by others, and chased away from the better feeding areas.

However, this type of guarded treatment of a new elk changes markedly if that cow happens to have a calf with her. Many times, I've seen a strange cow approaching a new herd who was met with wariness and hostility until her calf was spotted. Then the other elk seemed to lose their suspicion and doted on the calf, which also brought quick acceptance of the cow to the elk family. It is a wonderful sight in the elk herd to see even the most aggressive cows stop and take time to lovingly muzzle one of these helpless newborns.

Much of the enjoyment of watching a herd of cows comes from the variety of action among the animals. There always seems to be a few younger cows that are kicking up their heels and dashing through the elk herd with wild abandon while playing some type of elk tag. However, this exuberance is not shared by all the cows, and a younger cow that accidentally bumps into, or treads on the feeding area of, a surly older cow runs the risk of incurring her wrath.

Of course, an exception is made for the young. After a month of motherly doting, the calves begin to strike out on their own and act like most other youngsters. They constantly chase each other through the elk herd. Of course, that mean old cow that would severely punish a yearling for trespassing on her feed plot, stands by idly and watches the baby elk play. The calf elk are in constant motion, and the only time they slow down is when they get thirsty and drop by to nurse from mom, or fall exhausted to the ground for a short nap.

A large herd of cows amiably feeding in a lush high country meadow appears to be the epitome of peaceful coexistence to the casual observer. But upon closer inspection, life within the elk herd is rife with petty squabbles, and even contains its own loose pecking order. Much of the squabbling surrounds the best feeding areas. The older cows tend to chase away younger animals, and within that group of mature cows, there will be a few older animals who exert domination over most of the rest of the herd, if necessary. And within that inner core of dominant cows, there will be one cow, usually one of the oldest in the herd, which controls the actions and movement of the rest of the herd.

She is called the dominant, or lead, cow because she is usually in the lead. Her years of experience living in the same area helps her to lead the rest of the herd to the best sources of feed. And since she arrives there first, she also gets first feeding rights for the most lush, nutritious feed. And heaven help the foolish animal that infringes upon her feeding area. Immediately, the lead cow's ears lay

bull elk's loud, musical bugle not only serves to warn other bulls to stay away, but it so informs any receptive cow in the area that he is ready and willing to mate.

back, she extends her neck, and sends the trespasser on its way with a few vicious kicks with her forelegs.

After observing a herd of cows for a short period of time, dominant behavior and squabbles can be detected. Much of this is bluster and threat, followed by laid-back ears and false charges. However, physical confrontations are not uncommon among evenly matched elk. When this happens, both elk square off and eye each other, followed by the ears being laid back — a sure sign of pending aggression. If one of the cows does not back off, they raise up on their hind legs and flail away at each other with their hooves. Usually, the elk that lands the first of these sledgehammer-like blows sends the stunned victim running. At times, the lead cow will ignore such a squabble. At other times, she will intervene and stop the fight before it gets physical. But at other times, she may charge forward and pummel the cow that had just been victorious.

Cow elk emit a variety of sounds, and each sound has its own meaning, ranging from a cheerful greeting to a warning of danger. The most common elk sound in the herd is the cow call. This is a soft, nasal, musical sound of amiable greeting to others in the herd. In dense cover, cows are constantly "mewing" back and forth, as if to say, "Here am I; where are you?"

If a cow sees something that she cannot identify, but may be a source of danger, she emits a loud, shrill cow call. This instantly alerts the entire herd,

There are few sights in the natural world that compare to the peacefulness of an elk herd on a late summer evening feeding in an alpine meadow.

which ceases its meandering to stop and stare at the potential source of danger.

As soon as any member of the herd spots danger, such as a hiker or prowling lion, that elk will emit a loud, raspy bark. This sound instantly informs the rest of the herd that, indeed, there is something real out there to flee from. When the elk herd gets to this point, a stampede is imminent.

A fighting or angry cow emits a sound unique to that condition. She begins with a cow call, but then draws it out and raises its volume and intensity. This sound informs the elk around her that she wants space, or else! Two cows who square off to fight will approach each other while emitting the fighting cow call. When they rise up to flail at each other, the call evolves into a loud shriek. This squealing continues each time the cows rear up to flail at each other.

Cow elk do not bugle. However, a particularly exuberant cow emits a shrill, drawn out call that closely resembles the bugle of a young bull elk. A few years ago, I was photographing a herd bull that had a harem of ten cows tucked back into a small meadow hidden by a stand of dense fir trees. As I photographed the herd bull raking his antlers on a small pine tree, I heard what I believed to be the puny bugle of a spike or four-point bull. I expected the herd bull to suddenly charge after the young bull that had slipped in among his cows, so I was surprised when the herd bull ignored the call coming from the small meadow.

I was convinced that this sound was coming from a spike bull, so I sneaked

An immature bull that can't stand up to harassment from the older bulls usually joins a nearby herd of cows — as a subordinate.

over to the small meadow to take a peek at the lucky youngster that had somehow escaped the huge herd bull's wrath. I was surprised to find only cows and a few calves feeding and frolicking. Presently, a cow near me playfully chased another cow and then stopped and emitted this exuberant cow call that I'd mistakenly identified as a bull's bugle. Since then, I've heard this bugle-like sound several times among a herd of cows. It usually signifies a sense of well-being, even exuberance, among the animals in the herd.

There are few things in the natural world that I have experienced that compare to the peacefulness of elk country on a late summer evening when the elk herd is up and feeding in an alpine meadow. Calves are romping through the last rays of amber sunlight, as the cows emit a cacophony of calls which float almost musically through the thin mountain air.

Off by themselves on a distant ridge, a bachelor herd of bulls laze in the lush meadow grass, barely cognizant of the multitude of cows calling and milling in the distance. But there is also a slight chill in the evening air, with a somber hint of frost. And with the frost comes the elk rut. Soon, the bulls will take a keen interest in the elk herd.

Within the inner core of the elk herd, there is a group of dominant older cows. With that group, there is one dominant cow, called the lead cow. Her whims dictate the herd movements.

Chapter Nine

The Elk Rut

There is no other event in the outdoor world that compares with the elk rut for sheer drama and excitement. Like a strange metamorphosis, a bull elk changes almost overnight from a benign large deer into a snorting, frothing, vocal combatant. And if that wasn't enough, this entire intriguing ritual takes place in the breathtaking beauty of the pristine Rocky Mountains. In fact, the bugling cry of the mighty bull elk has come to symbolize all that is still wild and free in America.

Essentially, a bull elk's biological time clock begins winding down to the rut when the bull's antlers are shed in late April. Within a week, pulpy protrusions appear where days before there were only ugly sores. This is also the shedding time for the elk's winter coat, and during these spring months the bull elk hardly resembles the wilderness monarch he will become in a few short months.

Antler growth is rapid, and during this growing period, a bull is very careful to avoid damaging the tender velvet-covered antler shoots. This velvet covering over the growing antler bone is actually a thin skin with fuzzy membrane. Though a bull tries hard to avoid damage, there are too many trees and limbs to avoid scarring the antlers, especially as they increase in size to four-feet in width or more. (See Chapter Eleven for in-depth elk antler biology.)

It is interesting to note that elk antlers during this velvet growing stage are pliable and warm to the touch. I once visited a man who had a young bull elk as a pet. This man had raised the elk after taking it in as an orphan when its mother was hit by a vehicle. I slowly approached the bull and carefully put my hand on an antler. The velvet was downy soft to the touch, and I was surprised by the heat. The antler wasn't just warm, it was actually hot — probably the result of the overactive growing process necessary to create such large appendages in only a few months.

Velvet antler covering that has been nicked or torn will bleed and then crust over with a dark scab. These minor injuries heal quickly and do not affect the finished antler, but rather unique injuries do occur. I once saw a bull in velvet with a quarter inch stub of a limb protruding from a hole about eight inches above the base in his right antler. My guess is that sometime during this soft growing stage, the bull had impaled the stick into his antler and then broke it off.

e elk rut is one of the most electrifying occurrences in the natural world. Overnight,
bull elk changes from a large benign deer into a vocal, aggressive combatant.

Several hunters have told me about seeing a bull elk with a bullet hole through its antler. I'd always found that odd, considering the tendency of hard antler bone to shatter upon impact with a high powered bullet. I believe that most of these "bullet holes" that hunters find in elk antlers are the result of sharp, brittle sticks having been impaled into the antler during its soft velvet stage.

A bull's antler growth is rapid, and an observer can notice a daily increase in the size of an elk's antlers. Through June and July, a bull's main goal in life is to eat the most nutritious food and escape the hordes of blood-sucking horseflies that often make life miserable for all flesh in elk country. His life is serene and peaceful as he lazes around in a bachelor group with other bulls.

It must be remembered that the sole purpose of an elk's antlers is to aid him during his battles with other bulls in the near future. By late August, antler growth is complete, and a bull's biological time clock is about to ring. As antlers reach optimum growth, the production of calcium falls off, which triggers a small secretion of the male hormone testosterone from the bull's testicles.

The increasing flow of testosterone into the bull's blood system also acts to cut off the flow of blood to the antlers, effectively killing these appendages. The soft cartilage quickly hardens into brittle bone, and shortly thereafter, the velvet dies and begins to dry and peel. A bull elk will vigorously rub his antlers against saplings and large bushes to shed the dried velvet.

I found it curious that this newly shed velvet was never found on the ground at freshly rubbed trees. I discovered the answer one day in late August as I watched a young bull rub the velvet from his antlers. As soon as the antlers were rubbed free of the velvet, the bull promptly ate it! Actually, this makes a lot of sense because the velvet contains lots of nutrients.

When they are first exposed, the new antlers are a dull bone color, but soon become stained brown from tree pitch and vegetative juices. The result is a spectacular set of long sweeping antlers. A mature bull may have antlers whose main beam exceeds five feet in length, and the inside spread between antlers may measure four feet or more. The main beams are a rich chocolate brown in color, and the tines have a peeled-back, ivory colored hue. Truly, these are some of the most spectacular antlers grown by any beast in the world.

All summer long, the bulls have preferred the company of their own gender. But with the velvet off their antlers, the bulls become moody and reclusive. Suddenly, they have no use for each other. Older bulls chase off lesser bulls, and the younger bulls begin to prod and push at each other to show dominance.

The week before the rut begins is a strange one indeed. Meadows and parks that were recently dotted with elk are conspicuously empty. When cows are spotted, they seem preoccupied and nervous. The bulls are nowhere to be found. They are all back in their own secluded lairs feeling those first confusing, yet wonderful, stirrings of the rutting lust.

Trees that were carefully rubbed just a week ago to remove the velvet from antlers are now attacked with vigor. The bulls continue to punish saplings and

This large bull elk in velvet carefully protects his antlers from injury during their growi
stage. Velvet antlers are nothing more than soft cartilage with a fuzzy skin covering.
this stage, they are pliable and hot to the touch.

bushes until they work themselves into a frenzy. At this time they also roll in dust, or in their own urine, and they seek out wallows to flounder in the musty waters that contain the scents of other elk.

A bull elk during this pre-rut stage is both absurd and intriguing. A bull may stalk up to a small sapling, drop his antlers to a fighting position, and then begin a silly prancing dance around the tree in mock combat. He'll make false charges and hook his mighty antlers at an invisible enemy. He'll stop to feed amiably for a few minutes and then suddenly dash around in a wide circle kicking up his hooves and shaking his antlers at some unseen foe.

With each passing day, testosterone flows through the bull's system with dramatically increased frequency. Those wonderfully strange initial mating urges that the bull had experienced a week ago rapidly evolve into raging pangs of lust that threaten to consume his entire mind and body. And in the end, they do.

In every drainage, the scenario is the same. At first light on a crisp autumn morning, a lonely, high-pitched wail echoes through the high country like the cry of a wilderness ghost. A minute later another bugle sounds from a nearby ridge, followed by an answering call from a small meadow. Then another bull bugles, and another and another until the squealing challenges of bull elk ring through the mountains. It is the dawn of the rut.

During the early stages of the rut, many of the mature bulls begin bugling, but not herding cows. This usually occurs during the first week in September in the high country. Several times, I've spotted a mature bull elk tearing up trees and bugling at one end of a meadow while several uninterested cows fed a few hundred yards away and totally ignored the bull's antics.

During those early rut days, an immature bull may be seen with a small harem of cows, acting every bit like a mean old herd bull. That is, until the real thing shows up! Last fall I spotted a young four-point bull with four cows. I also spotted a huge six-point bull about eighty yards away in a creek bottom. For two days the big bull spent most of his time raking his antlers and sparring with saplings.

One morning while I was photographing the small herd bull, the big six-point bull appeared and came stomping in his direction. Moments before, that young bull was acting like the supreme lord and master of those cows, but he sheepishly trotted off and the big bull took his place as if on cue.

A herd bull will gather up as many cows as he can, and he'll run himself ragged constantly chasing away other bulls and rounding up wayward cows. Some harems exceed thirty cows, and keep the herd bull plenty busy.

Unfortunately for the herd bull, the actual mating act depends upon the cow. Coupling is impossible until a cow enters her estrus cycle. Beginning in late August, a cow elk will enter into estrus once every twenty-eight days. Of course, not all cows come into estrus at the same time, so the bull keeps them all packed into a tight herd, biding his time until each cow is receptive to mating. (See Chapter Eleven for cow elk estrus biology.)

There has been some misinformation in recent years concerning a mating sound, called a mating mew, supposedly made by a cow when she is ready to be

...en the dead antler cartilage hardens to bone, a bull vigorously rubs the velvet from ...antlers. At this time, he is ready to mate.

mated. I've watched at least twenty elk matings from close range, and I've never heard the cow emit a sound. Instead, the bull is attracted to the cow by the release of pheromones from her vagina when she is in heat and receptive. In fact, it is common to see a bull pursuing a cow closely with his tongue flicking in and out like a dog because he is literally "tasting" those juicy female in-heat hormones.

The typical scenario of a mating begins when the cow stops running away and allows the bull to approach her from the rear. If the bull is busy, I've seen cow elk back right up to the bull's chest, spread their rear legs slightly, and then glance back at him. But for all the fury and bluster of the rut, the actual mating process is brief. The bull hops up and holds the cow's rear haunches with his forelegs, then penetrates and ejaculates into the cow with one tremendous surge. That's it — over and done with! The bull then turns his attention to the next cow, but he will be back to mate that cow again, possibly three or four more times, during her relatively short period of estrus lasting about eighteen hours.

Wayward cows are dealt with harshly by the herd bull. I was quietly trailing a herd bull with a dozen cows last September during a photographing session, when the bull suddenly stopped and looked off to his right. The bull acted very agitated and charged over to a cow that had bedded down away from the herd. The bull prodded the chastised cow back to the herd with his long neck extended like

Even though a bull in rut is ready to mate, he must wait for the cows to come into heat. Until a cow reaches her estrus cycle, mating is impossible.

a big snake and his nose stuck up in the air.

A bull elk's main purpose in life is to mate, and the purpose of his glorious rack of antlers is to insure that the strongest mature bulls that are in their prime will pass on their seed. However, actual fights to the death are uncommon. Much of the pecking order among the bulls had been established in summer while the bulls lived in bachelor groups. Most of the fighting occurs between immature bulls that are experiencing those first wonderful pangs of rutting lust. Friendly pushing matches and clacking antlers are common among younger bulls.

That's not to say that the elk rut is a timid affair. As the rutting frenzy increases, bulls that knew their place a week ago, suddenly lose fear — and often their lives — when they do not retreat from the routing charge of the herd bull. A few years ago, I watched a big six-point herd bull three times put the run on a bachelor bull that was every bit as impressive in body and antler size. The first time, the bachelor bull trotted off. The second time he stomped off, but the third time he stood his ground and lowered his antlers.

Until then, I'd watched a few harmless pushing matches between lesser bulls, and I half expected the same thing. Not this time. The herd bull came at the bachelor bull in a crouched run with his neck extended and hair on end. The challenger arrogantly raised his snout and hissed back a warning. The herd bull

The herd bull jealously guards his harem of cows. While bachelor bulls may engage in friendly sparring, the herd bull will viciously attack and sometimes even kill any bull that roams too close to his cows.

slowed when he was fifteen yards away, and for a moment I thought it might end as a simple pushing match.

But then the herd bull's ears laid back, and the bachelor bull's did the same. I'd been around elk long enough to know what that meant! They stood eyeing each other for a few seconds. In a blur, a ton of fury met head on with a loud crash of antlers that actually shook the ground.

For a few seconds, the massive bulls strained mightily at each other, but then the bachelor bull began skidding backwards from the sheer brute force of the herd bull. The bulls spun around twice, and the herd bull succeeded in knocking the challenger off his feet. While the bachelor bull was still down, the herd bull twice viciously rammed his dagger-like antlers into the helpless bull's soft belly area. Finally, the bachelor bull regained his feet and fled, limping badly, with the herd bull giving chase.

I'll never forget the sight of that victorious herd bull standing there, head down and shaking his mighty antlers at the vanquished challenger. From that day on, the lame bachelor kept to himself in a thicket and seldom bugled. I later learned that Park rangers had found a mature bull elk dead in that area, and I'm sure it was the bachelor bull that was injured too badly to survive the rigors of winter.

Bull elk become totally consumed by the rut, and they eat very little during this period. The big herd bulls especially show a dramatic weight loss of up to 15 percent due to lack of food and the hectic routine of mating, rounding up wayward cows, and chasing off other bulls. The fat reserve that was built up during the lazy summer months sustains them, but later in the winter many of the older bulls have a difficult time surviving the harsh western winters with no fat reserve to carry them through the lean winter months.

Usually, by mid-October the rut has run its course. A few bulls may still bugle once in a while, but the harems have dispersed, and the intense rivalry between bulls has ended. To complete this awesome wilderness cycle, the bulls once again seek out each other's company and spend the rest of the winter in a lonely fraternity. The biological time clock is about to reset. Antlers will shed, new ones will grow, and next fall when the frost lies heavily on the autumn grass, the bulls will once again feel the fire in their loins.

hese two mature bachelor bulls began their sparring as a friendly pushing match, which uickly escalated into a fierce, bloody struggle.

Chapter Ten

Seasons Of The Elk

The elk herd exists in four distinct time periods during the year, which coincide with the seasons — spring, summer, fall and winter. Each season presents it own challenges for the elk herd, and offers specific insights into the ever-changing world of the elk.

Most folks visit elk country in either summer or fall, when the animals are at their best, and activity and vigor among the elk is at its peak. However, a true student of the natural world should plan a spring and winter trip to elk country in order to more fully understand the wondrous perfection of nature, even when that perfection comes at a seemingly unconscionable price.

Spring

Spring is a time for optimism throughout elk country. The long, harsh winter has finally ended, and the females of all species are heavy with young. Unfortunately, spring has two faces: one of renewal in late spring, and one of death in early spring.

In the natural world, spring begins when the snow disappears from the low country. The dull landscape begins to change color from drab brown to green as tiny shoots of grass are coaxed upward by the weak spring sun. Most of the elk herd hungrily devour these nutritious sprigs of grass. It's not unusual to find the elk on their knees with their snouts to the ground nipping the new grass when it is barely an inch high. These are the mature, strong animals in their prime that have come out of winter with enough stamina to quickly build up their depleted bodies.

Missing are many of the yearlings that had frolicked among the elk herd last summer. Their smaller size and lack of experience made them a winterkill statistic. Some of the older animals have survived the winter, but it has taken a toll on their bodies. Bulls and cows that had not been able to sustain a minimal amount of nourishment through the winter, have had the muscle and marrow devoured from within and now stumble around looking like hide-covered skeletons.

Even though the grass is green and other elk are finally nourishing their depleted bodies nearby, these sickly elk are too weak to compete or expend the extra energy required to nip the new shoots of grass. Instead, they stare glassy-eyed, or lie for hours as if napping peacefully, but their ghastly appearance tells even the casual observer that something is terribly wrong. At this point the elk is

*en though the snows are gone, some elk are
) weak to gobble up the nourishing spring
ass and thereby seal their own fates.*

virtually dead, though thin blood still weakly pulses through its body, and the best team of veterinarians in the world could not save it. It is in shock and its body has virtually consumed itself. Its not a pretty way to die, and at this stage, it's actually a relief to see a pack of wolves or a surly grizzly bear putting a needless sneak on one of these starved elk because I know that very soon their ordeal will end.

In Yellowstone Park, where an estimated 30,000 elk live, it is believed that anywhere from five to ten thousand elk die from starvation, depending upon the severity of the winter. This is part of nature's cycle that most animal lovers miss. When these nature lovers enter Yellowstone Park for a summer vacation in July, the dead elk have been removed or consumed, and they see only the pretty side of the wild kingdom complete with sleek elk and cavorting calves.

Actually, the person who views this low ebb of the elk herd and understands its purpose and necessity will not only have a better understanding of the cycle of nature, but also gain a greater appreciation for the life-giving sustenance and renewal that the death of one animal furnishes to another.

This was the philosophy that the Native American lived by. In his memoirs, Gray Wolf, a Blackfoot Indian, wrote: "When an Indian killed an animal, he performed a ceremony over the carcass and thanked the animal for giving its life so that the Indian's family could live. The Indian also assured the dead animal that he would use every part of the animal for food, clothing or tools."

By mid-spring, the elk have recovered sufficiently to begin the renewal process. The bulls have broken away from the main elk herd and have reacquainted themselves with others in bachelor herds, where they spend most of their time eating, sleeping and feeling the growth of new antlers.

There may also be sound biological and survival instincts that prompt bulls to congregate far from the herd of cows. Bulls tend to be surly, impatient animals, and a calf romping through a bull's space would probably be hammered by a bull that doesn't share or exhibit any paternal instincts. A cow elk is a very protective parent and is not above pounding on a bull that is mean to her baby, so it's a good reason for the genders to separate.

Also, the bulls know that the mighty grizzly bear is always around the cow

: elk herd exists in four distinct life cycles, which coincide with the seasons.

herd hunting for a calf, or even a mature cow, if it can get one. Instinctively, a bull elk knows it is no match for the power and ferocity of a grizzly bear, so the best place for the bulls to be safe is to live far away from the main elk herd where all the predators tend to congregate.

As the season progresses, the snow line recedes farther up the mountain, and the elk literally follow it up to the higher country. The new grass is surely one of the attractions, but the main reason is that elk like to live in seclusion, away from roads, houses, barking dogs and the prying eyes of humans. It is in these secluded high country basins where the cows seek out birthing areas, usually near dense cover where they can escape the ever-watching eyes of the predator during this short period when they are totally helpless.

When a cow elk knows that her time has come, she usually moves off by herself to dense cover or a small patch of brush where she can lie down without being seen. Within the hour, the calf is born. The cow immediately severs the umbilical cord and eats the afterbirth, which is not only nutritious, but also removes this telltale sign that a newborn elk is near.

The cow then rejoins the elk herd. It is amazing to view an elk herd in mid-June — and see twenty cows with no calves. The elk graze and laze for a couple of hours, and at first, you wonder if all the calves have been killed. But then you notice a cow here and there sauntering off for a few minutes into cover, before returning to the herd. What is not seen is that she nurses her calf away from prying eyes, and then makes sure that the calf lies down again in good cover before hurrying back to the herd.

After about a week, the calves have already gained enough strength to join the main elk herd, but they spend much of their time either bedded down close to mother or up and nursing. It is during this time period when the calves are most in danger from predators. Bears especially roam through these birthing areas and hunt much like a bird dog, roaming back and forth until they catch the scent of a newborn. They quickly follow the trail until the hidden calf jumps up and runs to join its mother. Initially, the calf's speed is surprising, and it outruns the lumbering bear for a few hundred yards, but a calf's stamina at this age is minimal, and soon the bear is speeding up, while the calf is slowing down.

One hammer-like blow usually all but kills the calf, and the bear then tears it apart while the hysterical mother is forced to watch nearby. Elk have an instinctive fear of bears, and it is almost impossible for a cow to confront a bear. However, I once watched an awesome example of communal protective elk motherhood. I'd watched as a 300 pound grizzly ran down a calf after scattering a herd of eight cows. The calf was crying out while lying under one of the grizzly's paws. The bear sat on its haunches resting for a minute after a particularly long chase.

Suddenly, four cow elk charged the bear, and the startled bruin jumped up and ran into the timber, with the cows in close pursuit. Unfortunately the calf was lame from the bear's initial attack and had trouble running. Not to be denied, the grizzly circled and rushed the calf again. This time the bear killed the calf quickly and dragged it into the trees before the cows could regroup. But even nature has

The exuberance of new life from a fresh calf crop is followed closely by a horrible killi
field when large predators move into the elk's calving areas to prey on the newborn

its ways of evening the score. A few minutes later, three gray wolves showed up and drove the grizzly from the kill, whereupon the wolves joyfully tore the calf apart.

Within three weeks, the calves are strong enough to outrun a bear. At this stage, the calves are a joy to watch as they prance and dance and chase each other around the woods. No doubt, wolves and grizzlies lying in concealing cover are able to pick off a few of these youngsters when they pass by. But for the most part, the calves are able to keep up with the cows and outrun most predators.

Summer

The summer season usually begins in late June when the elk eventually arrive, following the receding snow line, to the high country, where they spend the entire season lazing around and eating the nutritious grasses and browse flourishing everywhere in the moist high country basins where the deep snow has left the soil spongy and fertile.

Actually, this entire process of following the receding snowline makes sense because the elk will have benefitted from optimum nutrition furnished by the succulent young grass that emerged in a continuing line up the mountain just below the snowline. And now in summer, when the lower country grasses are shriveled and tasteless from burning under ninety degree heat and typical summer drought, the elk are gorging on vast profusions of juicy grasses and wildflowers.

Because of the higher altitude, the upper reaches of the mountains rarely even reach eighty degrees, while below the thermometer may hit a hundred. Also, the high country always has a steady breeze to cool off the elk and keep the bloodthirsty biting insects at least partially at bay.

The increased atmospheric pressure in the mountains creates a never ending succession of thunderstorms in the high country. No matter how bright and sunny most of the day may be, a late afternoon buildup of clouds appears in startling swiftness, and a violent storm complete with hurricane-like winds, tremendous peals of thunder and countless jagged tongues of fiery lightning are a common occurrence. During the worst storms, the elk will bed down facing away from the wind, but at other times, they ignore the storm and continue feeding through it.

During the transition from spring to summer ranges, the elk lose their ragged coat of dense hair and now look sleek in their brilliant dark rust colored summer coats. This short summer coat allows an observer to appreciate the sleek athletic physique of the elk. Its long slender rear legs rise up to huge, heavily muscled hams. The elk's longish body is a miracle of tight, sinewy muscles and bone. Its elongated, greyhound-type ribcage ends in a huge chest of muscle, bone and powerful dark brown forelegs. Its long neck appears both graceful and powerful and carries the elk's head in a stately position, as if the elk was aware of its regal appearance.

The calves have become much more independent and often stay away from their mothers for extended periods of time, where they group together, play and laze in the summer sun. But they are never out of their mother's sight, and they continue to seek her out for nursing duties every few hours. This nursing will

wborn calves lay hidden in brush most of their first two weeks of life and emerge only
ing their mother's frequent nursing visits.

continue into the fall, when the calf's size and rough treatment force the harried mother to finally wean the calf. But during these summer months, the cow is still the slave to the calf's demands.

The calves slowly begin to lose their spots by late summer. The spots change from almost white when first born, to pale yellow by late summer and begin to fade appreciably until it is difficult to see the spots on a calf at any distance, and it begins to resemble a miniature elk more and more.

Late summer brings the fullness of the seasons. Berries ripen and provide extra nutrition and fat gathering potential for all animals, including the elk. Elk especially like elderberries, commonly called "elk candy." Elk also dine on huckleberries, raspberries, serviceberries and wild currents.

However, the ripening of the berry crops also serves as a harbinger that the summer season has almost completed its cycle. Late summer days continue fair and balmy for the elk, but now at sundown there is a crispness in the air, and some of the low bushes up on the mountaintops have turned bright orange and red.

The cows instinctively feed more often, as do the bulls off in the distance in their bachelor herds. Fat is being stored for the lean winter months, and for the bulls, this may be their last chance to eat until their bellies are full. The seasons are about to change, and nothing will be the same again for them.

A calf elk in summer becomes more independent. When it's not suckling or sleeping, it's playing tag with the other calves.

Fall

In elk country, fall begins when the first frost appears, usually the beginning of September, and changes the soft dew into hardened ice. It is a dying time for the plant life, but you'd never know it from their last brilliant showing of colors. Weak green aspen groves turn overnight into dazzling seas of yellow and orange. Low brush and high bushes also exhibit a riot of colors that suggest a final celebration before their long period of naked slumber.

The bull's antlers have formed and are now shed of their dead velvet skin, revealing dead bone that is quickly stained brown from the bull's incessant raking of his antlers on brush and trees. The bachelor herds break up, and the bulls go their separate ways, feeling confused and tentative as the first minute levels of testosterone begin to change their personalities and priorities.

The frost burned grass in the alpine areas quickly withers and does not provide the best feed, so the cows move farther down the mountainside into the timber, where protected small meadows and parks still provide succulent grass. The bulls follow close behind, but contact with the cows is not immediately apparent.

The mature bulls, in response to the rapidly increasing testosterone level, go off by themselves to punish trees with their antlers. Younger bulls engage in

The summer season is a time of plenty, when tall grass provides much nourishment for the elk in their sleek reddish-brown summer coats.

joyful pushing matches and begin to prod at cows. They don't know exactly what they want, or even how to do it, but instinct tells them that the cows are the source of their pangings.

Of course, the cows ignore all of this sudden attention by the younger bulls. These immature bulls loosely "adopt" a herd of cows, sniffing and gesturing at the females, but generally, the cows do not come into heat until mid-September, almost two weeks after the bulls were ready. When the testosterone level finally gets a mature bull into a rutting frenzy, he begins seeking out herds of cows, and he usually takes over from a younger bull without incident.

If the foolish younger bull should drop his head to engage in a friendly pushing match with the oncoming mature bull, he quickly learns that a herd bull takes the rut seriously. I once watched a spike bull prance around a herd bull and his harem of cows, and it was obvious that he considered it a game to be chased by the herd bull. He'd sneak in among the cows and then prance away when the herd bull came charging after him.

Finally, the young bull became brazen enough to actually try to mount one of the cows. The herd bull went berserk and chased after the invader with startling speed. After a gallop of 200 yards, the young bull realized that this was not a game. The herd bull was almost on him when they disappeared over a ridge. I heard a tremendous commotion, and the herd bull finally stalked back to his herd. From that day forward, the young bull reacted like a frightened rabbit whenever another bull came into view.

In open country, a herd bull can control his harem of cows, but in heavy timber or brush, cows are continually wandering off. The result often leaves a resident herd bull with fewer cows than some of the inferior bulls that were lurking just out of sight.

One of the most interesting rutting encounters I've ever observed occurred two years ago near Banff, Alberta. The first day I arrived at a secluded meadow to photograph rutting elk, I discovered a huge bull with palmated antlers jealously guarding his harem of about thirty cows from four young bulls, plus one other huge bull who was equally as large as the herd bull. Several times, they met in that meadow and engaged in furious pushing matches, with the palmated bull eventually winning out.

But when I arrived at the meadow the next morning, it was the palmated bull who was without cows, and the six-point was the new herd bull. The next day, both bulls had their own herds at opposite ends of the meadow. As cows began to drift back and forth, the herd bulls became berserk with rage and engaged in several furious fights, with neither bull gaining the upper hand. Finally, the six-point bull pushed the palmated bull toward the edge of the meadow, broke free, and then quickly rounded up all of his adversary's cows and pushed them over to his herd. The palmated bull screamed insults and challenges at the herd bull, but then sulked off into the timber. I left the area after that, but it wouldn't have surprised me to have found the tables turned by the next morning.

By mid-September, the rut is at its peak, and there is a frenzy of activity as most of the cows come into heat during that week. The scene in elk country is

e fall season begins when the solitary bulls rub the velvet from their antlers and begin rching for receptive cows.

chaotic, as herd bulls chase down wayward cows, mate others, and then have to stop whatever they're doing to chase away bachelor bulls who are moving in on the fringes of the harem.

At this time, mature bachelor bulls, who just a week previously knew their place in the pecking order, are now so hopelessly consumed by the fires of the rut, that they risk death with the dangerous herd bull in desperate battles. Usually, the herd bull wins out, leaving the challenger limping and scarred. These mature bachelor bulls become so unpredictable that they often fight to the death among themselves, and they have been known to chase pack strings of horses that invade their domain. They've also been know to tree hikers and photographers (including myself several times).

By the first week of October, the rut has run its course. A few of the frustrated bulls that had no chance to mate are still occasionally bugling, but the harems of cows have begun to break up. By mid-October, bulls that were mortal enemies just a month ago, now seek out each other's company again. Most of these bulls are gaunt from too little feed and too much activity. Some are lame. Others nurse nasty gouges inflicted by an adversary's daggerlike antlers. The bulls seek out secluded areas to nurse their injuries and they spend most of their days feeding in an attempt to regain strength, weight and body fat because they know that the lean season is almost upon them.

Winter

Winter begins in elk country when the first snow arrives and stays. Snow squalls may hit the high country in early September, but soon melt off. By late October, snowfall in the high country increases and bare ground will not be seen again up there until the next June.

For the past seven months, life had been good for the elk. The feed was continually getting better and better, as they followed the snow fields and fed on the succulent new grasses. But now, those grasses are frost withered and buried under one, then two, then three feet of snow.

The pristine high country, after just one big storm, may become virtually unlivable for the elk. The elk begin a slow, steady descent down the mountain where snow depth is lower. Often times, they are able to drop down below the snow line and enjoy a few weeks of feeding on bare ground, but by late November, even these middle elevations now have a few feet of snow.

The elk move down farther, until they arrive at the lower elevations where snow depth usually does not exceed two or three feet all winter. Still, it is a challenge to exist for three months in three feet of snow. The elk exert much energy as they paw down through the snow to nibble at the shriveled strands of grass. Fortunately, elk have two chambers in their stomachs, and they are able to digest both grass and browse. When the snow depth makes grazing impractical, the elk turn to browse almost exclusively.

It has been said that elk are on a slow cycle of starvation as soon as winter arrives. The elk cannot sustain their weight and body fat while pushing through the deep snow and nibbling a few pounds of frozen bushes each day. Those elk that

The haunting, musical bugle of the bull elk in rut is full of fury and power. Sportsn and nature lovers come from all over the world to experience the elk rut.

are healthy and carry a good reserve of fat, can usually make it through the rigors of winter.

The most adversely affected are the young, the old and the bulls that rutted too long and hard. The first to feel the effects of winter's deprivation are the young elk. That year's calves are too small to be abe to reach high up in the brush and trees for browse when the lower levels are depleted. They also exert much more energy pushing through the deep snow. The older elk, even their mothers, chase them away from the dense thickets where the best browse is found.

The older elk whose age-related deficiencies, such as worn-down teeth and arthritis, slow them down, also begin to suffer as the winter deepens. The mature bulls who were in their prime just a few months ago, now desperately struggle to maintain their critical body weight. Even though the rut is past, they are not adverse to using their wicked antlers to chase younger bulls and cows away from the best feeding areas. But sometimes that is not enough.

By February, some of the younger elk are already beginning to fall behind. The older elk that are chased away from the best feeding grounds, also approach the point of no return. By March, when signs of spring are beginning to appear, many of these younger and older elk are walking zombies, oblivious to the world around them. They stumble through the snow without feeding, and they lay down

After the brief cohabitation with cows during the rut, those bulls that were just a few weeks ago engaged in deadly duels — now seek out each other's company during the stark winter months.

on bare ground without bothering to glean any old grass exposed by the receding snow. Their bodies have turned cannibal and begun to devour their muscles and bone marrow. They become light-headed and somewhat delirious, oblivious to approaching humans or predators. At this point, they are dead, but often lay gasping and wheezing for days. At this point, death by any means is a relief, and the winter killed elk becomes a source of life for a variety of predators and scavengers.

Conclusion

The seasons of the elk run the gamut, from an explosion of new life in spring, to the lonely, desperate struggle to survive winter. We humans are fixers, and we're always trying to fix with technology and science, what nature has provided as the best way to manage the species. Predators can be killed, poisoned and trapped to allow more calves to survive in spring, only to die off in winter if the carrying capacity of the land will not provide enough feed. The practical answer to man's involvement is to provide more critical winter habitat and also lessen the impact on the elk's winter range as much as possible through the careful regulation of housing subdivisions, ski resorts and heavy winter recreation activity.

The biggest bulls that rutted hard and fed little during the frenzied action of the rut now find themselves gaunt and haggard as the winter snow builds up.

Chapter Eleven

Elk Biology

The elk belongs to the *Cervidae* family, comprised of 53 species. The smallest member of this family is the ten-pound musk deer, while the largest member is the moose. More specifically, the elk fits in with the *cervus* lineage within the *Cervidae* family, of which there are fifteen species found in North America, Europe, Asia, East Indies and the Philippines. As detailed in Chapter Two, there has been a drawn out controversy about whether the European red deer and North American elk are, in fact, the same species. Currently, they are identified as close relatives. Today, the official scientific classification of the elk is *Cervus elaphus.*

Distribution

There are four subspecies of elk in North America. The most widely distributed subspecies is the Rocky Mountain elk, which is found throughout the Rocky Mountain states and accounts for about eighty percent of the total elk population. All of the recent transplanted elk have been Rocky Mountain elk.

The Manitoban elk is found mostly in Canada along the fringes between prairie and forest. There is some question whether the Manitoban elk is a pure subspecies today, after having been almost exterminated, and then freely intermingling with later Rocky Mountain elk transplants.

The Roosevelt elk is located along the rain forests of the Pacific Coast from northern California, through Oregon and Washington, and into southern British Columbia. Alaska also has a small Roosevelt elk population.

The Tule elk is found in small pockets throughout central California. This smallish elk is currently experiencing a population boom, and its numbers have more than doubled in the past twenty years. So have complaints from local farmers. As a result, a unique experiment using birth control to stabilize the Tule elk herd at a manageable size within its restricted environment has begun.

Physical Appearance

The elk has an elongated, deer-like appearance well suited for swift movement. But unlike the common whitetail deer, the elk's shoulders are much more muscular and pronounced. An elk's color tends to change with the seasons,

bull elk's testicles release testosterone into his blood, which eventually blocks the flow
blood to the antlers. These appendages quickly die and harden, whereupon the bull
bs off the velvet covering.

depending upon the growth stage of its hair. In spring, the heavy coat of dense hair which insulated the elk during the winter is a pale tan color. In late spring after the winter coat has shed, a new summer coat appears which is rusty tan in color. By August, the new coat has grown long enough to give the elk the classic tan color. Specifically, an elk's coloring is tan in the body, with a dark brown neck mane and head. Its lower legs are also dark brown.

Skeleton

The elk's skeletal configuration is elongated and narrow, which suits the elk well for running. Most of an elk's skeletal mass is formed within the first eighteen to twenty-four months of its life. A bull elk's skeletal mass will weigh about one hundred pounds, while the skeleton of a cow will weigh about eighty pounds.

Nutrition

A mature elk consumes about twenty pounds of feed per day under normal circumstances, or about two and one-half pounds per hundred-weight, to maintain and slightly gain weight. This volume may decrease if the elk is eating highly nutritious food in summer, while it may increase when the elk is eating dead grass or browsed twigs during winter.

Given the choice, an elk prefers to eat grass. However, in forested environments such as the dense rain forests along the Pacific Coast where little grass grows, elk feed is primarily browse. Elk in varied habitat feed on both grass and browse during the course of the day, but when both food sources are in abundance, the elk invariably chooses grass as its primary food source.

Dentition

Elk dentition is normal for the *Cervus* family of plant and grass eaters, with sharp flat front teeth for snipping off vegetation, and hard rounded molars for grinding it into pulp. Eventually, an elk's teeth wear down, and this fact, more than any other, limits the life span of an adult. Eight year old bulls have been killed who were in poor physical condition in places where nutritious feed abounded. Upon closer examination, it was discovered that their teeth were worn down below the gums, making it very difficult and painful to feed.

Digestion

An elk is classed as a ruminant, meaning that it has a rumen, or forestomach. (The rumen is the largest compartment in the four-chambered stomach.) Fortunately, the elk is among a select group of ungulates (plant eaters) that can successfully digest both grass and browse (twigs). This is due to the fact that swallowed food is stored in the rumen, where major nutrients are removed, and then regurgitated later when the elk is bedded. It is then chewed into fine particles and passed on to the stomach, where the rest of the nutrients are removed.

The rumen on an elk is not very large, so elk must feed about three times daily to sustain life. Usually, an elk feeds in early morning, beds down, then gets up and feeds again in mid-afternoon. The elk then beds, but returns to feeding again in evening. Consequently, when the elk is not up and feeding, it is bedded down and "chewing its cud" — the term which identifies the process by which the elk regurgitates and masticates coarse food into fine particles in preparation for passage to the stomach.

Diseases & Parasites

To the casual observer, elk look like they're always in good health, but it is unreasonable to think that the elk would be able to escape the ravages of disease and parasites. In fact, elk are susceptible to sickness and disease from a variety of disorders.

Diseases

Anthrax

Anthrax is a deadly disease that has killed untold millions of both humans and animals through the ages. Its source is a bacteria that occurs naturally in the soil. Unlike other maladies that infect slowly, and consequently are easier to treat, untreated anthrax causes a quick death. The infected dead animal then acts as host for countless millions of anthrax bacteria that can infect other animals that come in contact or inhale anthrax spores.

Much of the biology of the elk is fascinating to the elk lover. An in-depth knowledge of this animal allows an elk enthusiast to understand many aspects of the elk that the casual observer misses.

The scary thing about anthrax is that spores can lay dormant for years, and then when inhaled, they can become active and kill quickly. The good news is that there has been very little anthrax infection of wild elk. However, given the long term hibernation properties of this bacterium, and the fact that wintering elk often congregate in congested herds, an outbreak of anthrax has the potential to wreak havoc on an elk herd — and even humans who happen by.

Brucellosis

Brucellosis is a far more common and serious disease and currently infects many of our major elk herds. The wintering elk herd in Jackson Hole, Wyoming, was tested and found to have a fifty percent infection rate, while tests have also shown that many of the elk in and around Yellowstone National Park and western Wyoming carry the brucellosis virus.

Wildlife managers have been frustrated in their attempts to control brucellosis in the greater Yellowstone ecosystem because of the vastness of the elk and bison herds. One plan suggests that all the elk and bison in the infected Yellowstone area be killed and the brucellosis bacteria allowed to die off. As we have seen from the extreme adverse publicity when Montana agents killed infected bison that had wandered from the Park, this avenue should not be pursued.

These cow elk are filling their smallish rumens (forestomach). They'll soon bed down, regurgitate rough chewed food, and slowly pulverize it (chew their cud) into fine fiber before passing it on to the stomach.

Other plans call for vaccinations of entire herds, but the logistics of such a massive undertaking, and the almost certainty that some infected animals will escape the dragnet and reinfect the herd, keeps biologists scratching their heads on this disease.

Brucellosis is a much feared disease among cattle ranchers because it causes sterilization and abortions among female cattle. While many diseases are not, in reality, as dangerous as they sound, brucellosis remains a serious, but so far, unrealized threat to the elk herd.

Tuberculosis

The threat of tuberculosis in elk comes mostly from potential infection from wild animals that come in contact with diseased farm and game ranch animals. In recent years, several game farms in the United States and Canada have reported outbreaks of tuberculosis, and mule deer killed near infected game farms in Colorado and Wyoming, were found to have tuberculosis.

An outbreak of tuberculosis in Alberta game farms cost the province more than sixteen million dollars to quarantine and destroy 2,600 penned elk. Ten people were also treated for the disease, which was brought to the province from a Montana game farm. So far, twenty-six game farms in Alberta, and three in Manitoba, have tested positive for tuberculosis, and at least four elk exposed to the disease have reportedly escaped into the wild.

Due to the remoteness of most of these infected areas, massive infection and mortality of wild elk has thus far not occurred. But considering the fact that many scattered elk herds often congregate in winter range, game farm transferred tuberculosis keeps wildlife biologists nervous.

Necrotic Stomatitis

This disease, often called lump jaw, was once probably responsible for more disease-caused deaths among elk, and studies have shown that it had been the number one killer of elk at the National Elk Refuge in Jackson Hole, Wyoming.

Biologists who studied this disease in Jackson Hole discovered that the main culprit was hay containing the seeds of squirreltail grass, locally known as foxtail or bobtail barley. These sharp seeds often became lodged between the elk's teeth and caused cuts in the mouth lining, allowing this disease to enter the elk's body.

Essentially, necrotic stomatitis is caused by a bacterium called Bacillus necrophorus. Actually, it is a common organism found worldwide and is often present in an animal's mouth cavity and on vegetation.

Lump jaw occurs when the feed of the elk becomes coarse and causes cuts in the elk's mouth, allowing the necrophorus bacteria to enter the elk's body, where it flourishes and eats away the mouth and jaw bone.

The good news is that this disease has been virtually eradicated in Jackson Hole in recent years because herd managers have since gone to alfalfa pellets for winter elk feed.

However, lump jaw also occurs in the wild when elk become overpopulated and are forced to eat twigs of brush much larger than normal. When there is not enough feed in winter, elk often go back over the browse that had been fed on previously. Twigs up to a quarter inch in diameter are then chewed off the brush, but such large pieces of browse often cause cuts inside the elk's mouth. Also, elk who feed on rushes near hay meadows also tend to get cut mouths, and the incidence of lump jaw increases near these hay meadows.

The first indication of Necrotic Stomatitis in an elk appears as drooping of the ears, often including drooling and distended or lumpy jaws. Emaciation also becomes evident as the elk loses its ability to eat due to the huge sores and lesions inside its mouth, and the massive destruction of bone. At first, biologists were bewildered to find so many elk wasting away among the Jackson Hole herd when an abundance of hay was available, and the subsequent study and necropsies that were performed eventually brought to light this disease.

In summary, lump jaw is a disease of overpopulation and herd mismanagement. When the carrying capacity of the land is not abused by too many elk desperately chewing rough, course feed, Necrotic Stomatitis is not a serious overall problem in the herd.

Parasites

Several parasites also latch onto elk and use them as hosts. Arthropods such as ticks and mites are fairly common among elk. However, only the mite has the potential to cause serious harm to the elk. Massive infestations of the microscopic mites cause scabies, or mange, and pose a real danger to infected herds.

Mange

Mange is a relatively simple condition, but its effects can be deadly. As the mites burrow into the elk's skin, the animal rubs and chews at the irritated spots, which only creates open sores and breeding grounds for thousands of mites to hatch. Eventually, this process of rubbing and scratching causes massive scabs to appear which often cover most of an infected elk's body.

It is not unusual to find an elk with mange to be totally hairless and covered with scabs. I once viewed a magnificent bull elk that a hunter had harvested. The animal was huge and in the prime of its life, except that over half of its body had lost its hair and was covered with a hard crust of scabs.

An elk with a severe case of mange usually dies due to the opening of the body to infection and other diseases and parasites. And if the elk lives long enough to enter the cold winter months, it usually freezes to death because it has lost much of its hair.

The big problem with mange is that it often ravages an entire herd. However, that does not mean that every elk dies. Mange, in itself, is nothing more than an infestation of mites. Many elk who do not rub themselves totally raw often rid themselves of these microscopic pests when host conditions disappear.

Worms

Roundworms, lungworms, brainworms and arterial worms can also kill elk. Though mortality among elk is relatively low from these parasites, a few deaths are reported annually by biologists, and surely, some wild elk die unobserved. These parasites cause death by proliferating within the elk's body cavity and either congesting or consuming that area affected, which in turn causes death or leads to mortal conditions such as blindness or pneumonia.

Brainworm

The brainworm is the major killer of elk. However, scientists have discovered that brainworm affects mostly younger elk. After two years of age, brainworm death is relatively low.

The primary host of the brainworm is the common snail. Elk that ingest forage where the snail slithers pick up the larvae. These larvae find their way to the animal's spinal cord and travel up it to the membrane of the brain, where they consume brain tissue. The resulting damage is irreparable.

The eastern whitetail deer is a primary carrier of brainworm. Though they are resistant to high mortality from it, other species in their range, such as caribou, blacktail and mule deer, moose and elk, have experienced significant mortality.

Brainworm infestations have cropped up rather extensively in recent eastern elk transplants and have already caused a few deaths, leading some biologists to wonder if the extinct Eastern elk may have built up a natural immunity to the brainworm parasite.

Arterial Worm

The arterial worm is most prevalent where mule deer and horseflies exist

To the casual observer, elk always appear healthy, but it is unreasonable to think that elk would be able to escape the ravages of disease and parasites. This young elk is in poor physical condition, undoubtedly the result of some unseen disease or parasite.

in abundance along with elk. The arterial worm travels to an elk's head area and there produces larvae, which damage the head, ears, antlers or muzzle areas by consuming and blocking off arterial passages. While not always fatal, arterial worms cause disfigurement and damage which may ultimately lead to death.

Lungworm

The lungworm larvae are usually ingested with the elk's forage and travel up to the elk's lungs. Lungworm larvae create an elk's serious condition when they proliferate inside the lungs and cause irritation and inflammation. An infected elk may wheeze or cough, and its breathing may be labored. Death is usually from pneumonia caused by the above conditions in the lungs.

Gastrointestinal Worms

Several types of intestinal parasitic worms can infect elk. However the cold ground of the Rocky Mountain elk is not a good host habitat for most of these worms, so infection of these elk is minimal. However, in the moist, temperate rain forests of the Pacific Coast, intestinal worm infestations among Roosevelt elk is a serious problem.

Most of the Roosevelt elk in this moist climate carry this parasite. Some

A cow elk comes into heat about the middle of September in most of elk country. Before she reaches her estrus cycle, female hormones appear in the cow's urine and signal her upcoming heat cycle to a nearby bull.

deaths directly attributable to intestinal worms have been reported, but surely the poor condition of severely infected animals also leads to mortality from other sources. Biologists have attempted to treat artificial feed furnished to overpopulated wintering elk herds, with marginal success. The chemical that kills these worms, when applied to alfalfa pellets, repelled all but the most desperate elk. As a result, gastrointestinal worms continue to be a mortality factor among overpopulated Roosevelt elk herds.

Antlers

One of the identifying characteristics of members of the Cervidae family is the existence of a crusted antler base, called the pedicle. The pedicle is the central growing point from which antlers appear. Surprisingly, antler development can only be activated by the male hormone testosterone, which is why female elk do not grow antlers.

Shortly after a bull elk sheds his antlers, the inner core of the pedicle will appear as a bloody sore. Within days, the release of a minute amount of testosterone, produced by the testicles, triggers the body to produce a tri-calcium phosphate consisting mostly of calcium, phosphorous, sodium and potassium into the blood, which eventually make their way to the base of the pedicle and there begin to coagulate and build up.

As the new antler begins to grow, tiny corkscrew-like capillaries are formed within this loose cartilage matrix and wind their way up through the emerging antler. A soft, velvety covering of skin protects the new antlers, and at this stage, an elk's antlers are actually pliable and warm to the touch.

Contrary to popular belief, a bull elk cannot be force fed antler growing chemicals such as calcium or phosphorus. Antler growth is solely dependent upon the size of the pedicle, which determines the circumference (mass) of the antlers, and the bull's body size, which furnishes a specific flow of blood to the antlers. Bull elk that are force fed calcium supplements do not grow larger antlers because the regulated blood flow can only carry so much calcium fiber, and the excess that was introduced into the bull's system will be either used to nourish his skeletal system or voided from his body. In other words, large antlers cannot be created, they must be grown by mature bull elk whose bodies are large enough to supply the necessary nutrients for optimum antler growth.

Generally, a bull's antlers take about 130 days to grow to maturity, though a younger two and one-half year old bull may grow his antlers in about one hundred days. During the second half of this growing process, slight hardening of the outer shell of the bull's antlers begins, though the centers are still mostly pliable calcium fiber. When a bull's antlers have reached their optimum growth, an increase in the testosterone level actually causes clogging of the bone matrix at the base of the antlers and eventually kills them, leaving dead bone, which quickly hardens.

This deadening sensation probably triggers an instinctive reaction because a bull quickly rubs the dead velvet off his antlers, usually within an hour or two, and it also begins the staining process which will color the antler. Bulls that rub their antlers on trees with high pitch content, such as spruce or pine, often have very dark, almost black, colored antlers. Antlers rubbed on brush or fir trees tend to have a lighter brown color. Elk in captivity that have no vegetative source, usually rub on poles and other artificial objects, but their antlers remain a sickly bone color.

Cow Elk Estrus Cycles

No matter how sexually stimulated a bull elk may be during the rut, mating is impossible until a cow elk comes into her estrus cycle. Until then, a bull elk may nudge, mount, and even insert his penis partially into the cow's vagina, but copulation is not possible for two reasons. First, the vagina is too shrunken and dry to accept the penetration of the bull's penis. Second, a cow elk's vaginal mucus is normally too thick to allow a bull's sperm to penetrate far enough into the uterus to enter the ovaries. It is only during the cow elk's estrus period that the elasticity and fluidity of the vaginal mucus becomes thinned out enough to allow individual spermazoa to swim forward.

Cow elk begin to ovulate at about six months of age, which means that a female calf is safe from the berserk thrusts of a huge bull elk. However, a yearling cow elk can and will reach estrus. Unfortunately, it is not unusual for a yearling cow to lose her calf due to an inability to care for the newborn, or due to complications from an immature female reproduction system.

During the frantic action of the elk rut, it is difficult to identify certain specific female conditions that exist among the cow elk, but scientists have determined that the elk rut, at least on the female's part, is not only complicated, but is also very tenuous.

In game farms, a cow elk may come into her estrus cycle at any time. One game farm manager told me that his oldest cow always came into heat, and was mated, in February. However, in the wild, cow elk come into estrus in fall, usually in mid-September. This is nature's way of insuring the calf elk's best chance of survival due to optimum climate and feeding conditions during the warm summer months.

Pregnancy lasts about eight months, with calves being born usually the first week in June. Healthy cow elk under controlled conditions have been known to produce calves regularly to twenty years of age or longer. However, cow elk in the wild are susceptible to the ravages of disease and winter, and usually don't live beyond fifteen years.

During the early stages of the elk rut, it is not uncommon for a cow elk to come into silent heat. This condition exists when the cow ovulates and secretes another female hormone, progesterone, which in turn induces the secretion of pheromones from the cow's vagina and urine. These pheromones cause the bull to become sexually awakened by that particular female. This condition is called silent heat.

During this silent heat period, the bull will nuzzle the cow and attempt to mount her, but she usually flees. However, this chasing and sexual attention, plus occasional aborted mountings and insertion of the penis into the vulva (outside of the vagina), may actually serve to induce the cow to come into heat and begin her estrus cycle.

A cow elk's estrus cycle begins when an increased level of estrogen causes the mucus membrane to become elastic and more fluid, and the cow not only allows, but invites, a bull to mate her. When in full estrus, I've more than once observed a cow elk step into a bull's path, turn her rump to him and then slightly spread her rear legs. If the bull does not mount her immediately, the cow again backs up against the bull's chest, and she looks back at him.

However, the estrus cycle in a cow elk is short, only about eighteen hours. During this period, the bull may mount that particular cow several times, while also servicing other cows who may have come into heat. Usually, a cow elk is not selective, and a bachelor bull who is able to slip in among the herd may actually mate a cow in heat while the herd bull is busy tending other cows.

In a well regulated elk herd which contains mature bulls, a mature cow elk usually flees or kicks out at the attentions of a young bull. However, in elk herds where the bull/cow ratio is very low, or where mature bulls are not present, a mature cow elk will accept mounting from a lesser bull. In fact, in some areas which have been overhunted, harems with a spike bull at the helm have been observed.

Generally, the majority of cow elk enter their estrus periods during the middle of September, but if a cow does not become pregnant during her first estrus cycle, she will come into heat again in about twenty to twenty-five days. It is important to remember that the timing of the estrus period among cow elk is very little understood with respect to timing. This is one of the reasons why the elk rut often seems confusing, with bulls bugling madly in late August (because some of the cows came into heat early), and then other elk herds starting up the rut again in mid-October (because some cows entered their second estrus cycle when they weren't impregnated the first time).

Chapter Twelve

Elk Distribution and Top Viewing Areas

ELK DISTRIBUTION

Most of the million elk in America are found along the Rocky Mountain Front, with another large population of elk also residing in the Coastal Mountains of the Pacific Ocean. However, there is also a smattering of elk herds in fourteen other states and Canadian provinces stretching all the way back to the Atlantic Ocean.

The Rocky Mountain elk inhabits the Rocky Mountain states, plus the Cascade Mountain Range in Oregon and Washington. The Roosevelt elk is found along the Pacific Coast. Transplanted elk to the East have been mostly Rocky Mountain elk, though a few states and provinces also harbor the Manitoban subspecies, once thought to be extinct, but now considered largely incorporated into the Rocky Mountain elk's bloodlines.

Alaska

Surprisingly, Alaska has a small herd of about 1,200 Roosevelt elk. Most of these animals are found on Afognak Island, which was planted with elk in 1929. A few smaller herds are also located in Southeast Alaska's Prince of Wales-Outer Ketchikan County. Most of this habitat is dense rain forest, so the brush-loving Roosevelt elk is right at home.

Arizona

There are about 55,000 Rocky Mountain elk found mostly in the rugged Grand Canyon/ Mogollan Rim country of central Arizona running diagonally down through Cococino, Yavapai, Gila, Najavo, Apache and Greenlee counties.

Arkansas

Arkansas has about 450 elk in the northwest counties of Carrol, Boone, Newton and Searcy. These are transplanted Rocky Mountain elk from a 1981 transplant along the Buffalo National River. Elk were introduced to Arkansas back in 1933, but massive poaching and loss of habitat eliminated the elk from this state for almost fifty years.

•st of the one million elk in America are found along the Rocky Mountain Front and Pacific Coastal Mountains. However, a smattering of elk also inhabit five Canadian •vinces and fourteen other states.

California

California has about 9,000 elk combined from three subspecies: Roosevelt, Rocky Mountain and Tule. There are about 4,500 Roosevelt Elk located mostly along the northern Pacific coast Mountains in Del Norte, Humboldt and Siskiyou counties. A small herd of about 1,500 Rocky Mountain elk is located at the southern tip of the Cascade Range in northeast Modoc County. About 3,000 Tule elk are scattered throughout several west-central counties from Mendocino all the way down to Santa Barbara. One of the favorite elk viewing spots is at Point Reyes National Seashore just fifteen minutes drive from San Francisco.

Alberta

Alberta holds about 25,000 Rocky Mountain elk. The greatest populations are located along its western border where the Rocky Mountain Front runs. A few scattered herds of elk are also found in the southeast and central areas of this province.

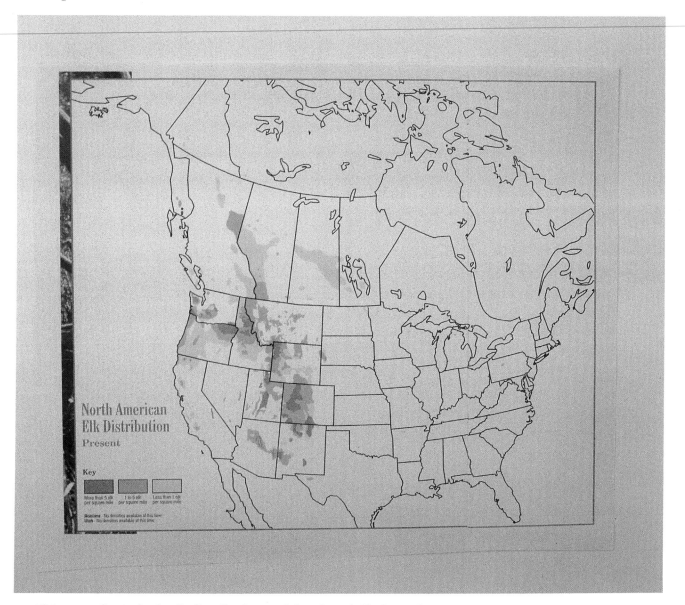

This map shows both elk distribution and density of elk throughout its present range. Map courtesy of RMEF.

British Columbia

British Columbia has about 50,000 elk, mostly located along the Rocky Mountain Front on its eastern boundary. In addition, there is a smaller population of Roosevelt elk along the southern Pacific Coast and on several larger islands.

Colorado

Colorado is tops with a whopping herd of about 250,000 Rocky Mountain elk. In fact, biologists believe that this state has exceeded its elk carrying capacity and plans are being made to reduce this huge herd. Most of the elk are located in the Rocky Mountain Front of western Colorado. In fact, elk are found in every county west of Denver. In addition, there is a small herd of elk located in Baca Country at the southeast tip of the state.

Idaho

Idaho has about 120,000 Rocky Mountain elk spread evenly through the Rocky Mountains along its eastern border. However, elk distribution also spreads far to the west and includes most of north and central Idaho. The only counties with no elk are the desert counties of Canyon, Owyhee, Twin Falls, and Cassia.

Kansas

Kansas has about 160 Rocky Mountain elk located in northeast Riley County. Another small herd lives in the southwest county of Morton. These are all recent transplants.

Kentucky

Kentucky has a newly transplanted elk herd of about 200 animals on reclaimed mine property in the eastern part of the state. Eventually, biologists hope to improve this seed herd to about 2,000 elk.

Manitoba

About 10,000 Manitoban elk are located in several pockets of suitable habitat in the southwestern corner of the province.

Michigan

Michigan has a healthy herd of about 1,500 Rocky Mountain elk located in the northern counties of Cheboygan, Presque Isle, Otsego and Montmorency. These are transplants dating back 30 years.

Minnesota

Minnesota has only a trace population of about 40 Rocky Mountain elk located in the northern counties of Marshall and Beltrami.

Montana

Montana has about 100,000 Rocky Mountain elk located mostly along both sides of the Rocky Mountains and west to the Idaho border. In addition, there are good elk numbers found in the Little Belt and Snowy Mountains of Eastern Montana. Elk are also slowly finding their way back to many eastern prairie counties where they once were historically abundant.

Nebraska
Nebraska has about 200 Rocky Mountain elk located in the northwest counties of Sioux and Dawes. These are recent transplants.

New Mexico
New Mexico has about 55,000 Rocky Mountain elk, with the majority located in the extreme northern counties. There is another large elk herd located in the far west counties of Catron, Grant, Socorro and Sierra. Another large elk herd is found in the southern counties of Lincoln and Otero.

New York
Though no elk exist in this state today, extensive studies are underway to explore the potential for introducing elk to the huge Adirondack State Park, most of the southern Catskill Mountains Park and surrounding portions of Allegheny and Cattaraugus counties.

North Dakota
North Dakota's elk herd numbers about 700 Rocky Mountain elk. Most of the elk are located in the extreme northeast counties of Pembina, Walsh and Cavalier. Another small herd lives in Bottineau and Rolette counties in the north, and another small herd is found in McKenzie and Dunn counties in the west. These are recent transplants.

Northwest Territories
A very small herd of about 20 Rocky Mountain elk inhabit a small area of suitable habitat in the extreme southwest corner of the province. This is the northern range of the elk.

Oklahoma
Oklahoma has about 1,000 Rocky Mountain elk located in the southwest counties of Kiowa, Caddo and Comanche. These elk are transplants from 30 years ago.

Ontario
Ontario has only a trace population of about 50 elk in the south. A study is underway to determine why elk have not prospered in Southern Ontario.

Oregon
There are about 130,000 elk in Oregon. About 65,000 Rocky Mountain elk inhabit the northeastern corner of the state. Another 65,000 Roosevelt elk live in the rain forests and Coastal Mountains along the Pacific Coast.

Pennsylvania
Pennsylvania holds about 340 elk in the central counties of Cameron, Elk, Clinton, Centre and Clearfield. Several state parks and forests provide both

security and feed in these counties.

Surprisingly, these are not recent elk transplants. A small elk herd had been transplanted to the Keystone State back in early 1900, but crop damage by the elk led to massive killing by both farmers and hunters, as well as poachers. However, a remnant of this old elk transplant somehow managed to exist through the decades and provided the seed for today's flourishing elk herd.

Saskatchewan

Saskatchewan has about 11,000 elk located in a band across the southern portion of the province. A few small elk herds are also found scattered along the southern border.

South Dakota

There are about 3,500 elk in the Black Hills along the western border counties of Butte, Lawrence, Pennington, Custer and Fall River. These are transplants from a few decades ago.

Texas

Texas has about 300 elk located in the western counties of Hudspeth and Culberson. These are recent transplants.

Utah

Utah has about 65,000 elk scattered through the Wasatch Mountains running north and south through the center of the state. In addition, several other large elk herds are scattered throughout Southern Utah where habitat is suitable.

Virginia

Virginia tried several elk transplants between 1910 and 1970, without success. Though no elk exist in Virginia today, studies are underway to explore the potential for restoring the elk to this state.

Washington

Washington harbors about 65,000 elk. About 30,000 Rocky Mountain elk are located along the eastern front of the Cascade Mountains in Central Washington, with another large herd located in the extreme southeast corner of the state. About 35,000 Roosevelt elk inhabit the forested terrain on the west side of the Cascades all the way to the Pacific Coast.

Wisconsin

Wisconsin has a very small elk herd of 30 recent elk transplants located near Clam Lake and in the northern counties of Ashland, Bayfield and Sawyer.

Wyoming

Wyoming's elk population numbers about 110,000 animals. The greatest concentration is in the western side of the state, especially south of Yellowstone National Park. However, there are also scattered elk herds throughout the state where suitable elk habitat exists.

Yukon Territory

A small elk herd of about 100 elk eke out an existence in a few suitable areas in the southern portion of Yukon Territory. This harsh land is the extreme northern range for elk.

TOP ELK VIEWING AREAS

While every state or province that holds elk offers the potential for viewing these animals, several specific areas in the West offer the best opportunity to see large elk herds under natural conditions. Most of these areas are located in national parks and provide an excellent vacation destination for the wildlife viewer.

Grand Teton National Park, Wyoming

Grand Teton National Park has not only elk, but also some of the most breathtaking mountain scenery in the West. The huge Teton Mountains rise all the way up to the clouds and create a fantastic background for photo bugs, who like to compose images with the peaks set in the background, and herds of elk grazing among a carpet of wildflowers in the foreground.

Both elk and moose are frequent roadside visitors along U.S. Route 287. In addition, the National Elk Refuge lies at the southeast end of Grand Teton Park, along U.S. Route 89. The Elk Refuge has several interpretive and visitors centers to help folks better understand the relationships between elk, habitat and people.

Most elk enthusiasts opt to visit the sister parks of Grand Teton and Yellowstone on the same vacation because the parks are only twenty miles apart. There may be more elk in Yellowstone, but the combination of remarkable alpine scenery and nearby elk make Grand Teton Park a must for western vacationers.

Jasper National Park, Canada

This Canadian Park is located along the borders of British Columbia and Alberta. Spectacular scenery and abundance of wildlife make this one of the most enjoyable and exotic parks for wildlife enthusiasts.

The town of Banff at the southern end of the park has many elk living around town, and they often feed along roads right at the edge of town. Elk viewing is also good along Route 93 north to Jasper. Large elk herds roam along the highway near Jasper.

During the rut, expect to see bugling bulls roaming along roadside and through openings just about anywhere out of Banff. The best elk rutting action near Jasper is found around town, and also along Route 16 east for about twelve miles.

The Whistler Campground at the southern edge of Jasper is aptly named. Campers are treated to a cacophony of bugling elk roaming through this campground through the night.

National Elk Refuge, Wyoming

The National Elk Refuge was created back in 1912 to accommodate huge elk herds that migrated to this low land from distant high country where deep

Several eastern and midwestern states now have small, but flourishing, elk herds than to recent transplants.

snow made life impossible. Today, the Elk Refuge accommodates more than 14,000 wintering elk from surrounding national forest, Grand Teton National Park, and even Yellowstone National Park seventy miles away.

This is an awesome winter vacation destination. Nearby Jackson, Wyoming has great skiing and unique western shopping. Elk viewing is from January through March, when the elk are amassed and fed at an annual cost of $350,000 to provide each elk with about eight pounds of alfalfa pellets daily.

This is a sight every elk lover should behold. The favorite method of viewing the elk is on a horse drawn sleigh provided commercially. These sleighs move right in among the thousands of elk concentrated in feeding areas. It is an unforgettable experience to be within arm's length of hundreds of bulls and cows, which ignore the horses and sleighs slowly moving through this vast elk herd.

The Rocky Mountain Elk Foundation has cooperated with the Elk Refuge to develop a comprehensive series of educational displays, along with visitor information services, to accommodate the nearly 300,000 people who visit the National Elk Refuge annually. The information center will aim to engage the visitor's interest in relationships among wildlife, habitat and people.

This is a winter elk viewing destination. The elk begin migrating back up to the high country by April, with only a few elk to be seen in this area by summer.

Rocky Mountain National Park, Colorado

Rocky Mountain National Park is not the best known park, but it is one of the top elk viewing parks in the West. This park is located just thirty-five miles north of Denver. Take the Loveland exit west from Interstate 25 and follow Route 34 for about thirty miles.

This beautiful park features a plethora of alpine scenery, along with a variety of wildlife. However, elk are the predominant species. Elk can be viewed just about anywhere in this park, but the best elk viewing is at the Alpine Visitor Center on Route 34. There is also an alternative one-way gravel road route to the Alpine Visitor Center that follows the Fall River. (It's called the Old Fall River road.)

If you drive Route 34 to the Alpine Visitor Center, park there and walk the Old Fall River road east for a few hundred yards. You'll be thrilled by the sight of hundreds of grazing elk in this high country paradise. This is the best place in the West to view large bachelor herds of velvet antlered bulls who have separated themselves from large nearby groups of cows and calves. Late summer is the best time to visit the Alpine Visitor Center. In fall, the elk move down to the lower country, where elk enthusiasts can view the excitement of the elk rut near any road.

Yellowstone National Park, Montana & Wyoming

Yellowstone is not only a great park to vacation at any time of the year, but it's also a wonderful place to watch wildlife during all seasons. In winter, the drama of the elk's survival is startlingly apparent as they eke out an existence in this deep snow country. In spring, the excitement of calves born in late May is often intensified by the drama of wolf and bear depredation. In summer, elk can be seen everywhere in huge herds out on open parks. In fall, the fantastic elk rut can be viewed from any road, as the bugling bulls roam freely through campgrounds, villages and across roads.

The good news is that this is "not" a destination where you hope you might get lucky and spot a few elk. On the contrary, elk are everywhere! Almost 35,000 elk call Yellowstone home, and virtually every sidehill or park opening is dotted with these magnificent beasts.

Top elk viewing is found near Gardiner and Mammoth Hot Springs on Route 89 at the northern entrance. Large elk herds can also be seen along Route 212 west from Mammoth Hot Springs toward Cooke City. The Lamar Valley is especially exciting because visitors often see wolves and grizzly bears hunting the vast elk herds roaming this valley. To the south, you can see lots of elk and other wildlife along Route 20 from Canyon (especially Dunraven Pass) south to Yellowstone Lake, and east to Norris and West Yellowstone. Route 287 past Old Faithful is another good place to see elk grazing in meadows.

Author's Note

Glacier National Park, Montana, is one of this country's premier national parks. It contains much breathtaking alpine scenery and trails, along with many thrilling opportunities to watch mountain goats and bighorn sheep. In addition, there are both black and grizzly bears in abundance.

However, Glacier National Park is a poor place to view elk. This Park is mostly high alpine terrain with dense forest below. There are only a few small elk herds scattered along the outer fringes of the Park. Consequently, this would be a great Park to experience high country wildlife, but it's not great for elk viewing.

THE ELK MYSTIQUE

Additional copies of *The Elk Mystique* can be obtained from many bookstores, sporting goods stores, other outlets, or directly from the publisher at Toll Free Number 1-800-735-7006. Other books by Mike Lapinski are also available, including *High Pressure Elk Hunting,* the *Western Hunting Guide,* and *Radical Elk Hunting Strategies.*